A FL

CW00505987

O Thou who camest from above
    The pure, celestial fire to impart,
Kindle a flame of sacred love
    On the mean altar of my heart.

Charles Wesley, 1762

The Society was all in a flame of love.

Charles Wesley's Journal,
11 July 1751 at Darlaston

A FLAME OF LOVE

A PERSONAL CHOICE
OF CHARLES WESLEY'S VERSE

———

TIMOTHY DUDLEY-SMITH

First published 1987
Triangle
SPCK
Holy Trinity Church
Marylebone Road
London NW1 4DU

British Library Cataloguing in Publication Data

Wesley, Charles
    A Flame of Love : A personal choice of
    Charles Wesley's verse.
    1. Wesley, Charles — Criticism and
    interpretation   2. Hymns, English —
    History and criticism
    I. Title   II. Dudley-Smith, Timothy
    264.2'0924   PR3763.W5

        ISBN 0-281-04300-0

Typeset by Rowland Phototypesetting Ltd
Bury St Edmunds, Suffolk
Printed in Great Britain by
Hazell, Watson Viney Ltd
Member of BPCC Group
Aylesbury, Bucks

CONTENTS

Introduction   vii

1   Christ in Experience (1–20)   1

    Conversion to Christ · The eternal Son
    Christ our Redeemer · Christ our Advocate
    Christ our King · Christ in the heart

2   The Christian Year (21–46)   29

    Advent · Christmas · The New Year
    The Transfiguration · The Entry into Jerusalem
    The Upper Room · Passiontide · Easter · Ascension
    Pentecost · Trinity · The Meeting of Friends

3   Seven Psalms (47–53)   53

    Psalm 23 · Psalm 40 · Psalm 45 · Psalm 51
    Psalm 70 · Psalm 117 (1739) · Psalm 117 (1743)

4   Church and Ministry (54–75)   67

    The Church of God · Ministers of Christ
    God's invitation · The Lord's Supper

5   The Life of Faith (76–107)   91

    Penitence · Grace and salvation · Trust in God
    Abiding in Christ · Following Christ
    Trial and temptation · The Christian warfare
    Prayer and the Scriptures · Love, joy, peace
    Praise and thanksgiving

6   One-minute Meditations (108–117)   125

    On some words of Scripture

7   Each Returning Day (118–131)   131

    The new day · Grace at table · Daily work
    In a storm · The child and the family
    Music · Evening

8   Death and Heaven (132–138)   149

    Friends above · For one departing
    Condemned prisoners · After the funeral
    Rejoice for a brother deceased
    Lines dictated on his death bed · A Christian's epitaph

Index of Titles and First Lines   157

INTRODUCTION

Week by week, across the English-speaking world, we sing (I believe) more hymns by Charles Wesley than by any other hymn writer.

I can produce no evidence for this and in the nature of the case it would be hard to come by. For what it is worth, it is certainly my own experience as I visit a variety of churches; and as I look at the contents of current hymnals from this and other parts of the world. Isaac Watts is perhaps not far behind ('the gate that Watts had opened Wesley joyously entered' wrote Erik Routley) and in some Anglican circles J. M. Neale may be a more prolific contributor – but Charles Wesley's place in contemporary hymnody is, I believe, unmatched.

This is in part, of course, because of the sheer volume of his work. Dr Frank Baker calculates that he wrote *on average* ten lines of verse a day for fifty years – completing an extant poem every other day. No wonder, therefore, that Dr Baker speaks too of 'MS sources richer and more complicated than for any other poet'. But quantity alone would not ensure survival. For all his characteristic style, archaic in places to modern ears (language does not stand still during two centuries), Charles Wesley speaks to us today because he sings of a God who is timeless and therefore our Contemporary, of a Jesus Christ who is 'the same yesterday, today and for ever'. If it is the task of a hymn writer to offer to a congregation words in which to express the movements and aspirations of their hearts, then Charles Wesley at his best is still unequalled in fulfilling that commission. I venture to think, also, that it is due to him more than to any other man that the use of the hymn book in private devotion is still practised, and valued by those who practise it.

Charles Wesley was born in 1707, eighteenth child of Samuel Wesley, Rector of Epworth in Lincolnshire. He was King's Scholar and Captain of Westminster School, graduating from Christ Church, Oxford in 1730; the value of his classical training in rhetoric, grammar and logic has been plainly demonstrated by students of his verse, which was classical before it was Christian. He was ordained by the Bishop of London in 1735, joining his brother John in the mission to Georgia as Secretary to the Governor. This appointment was short-lived; and he was soon back in England, teaching English to Peter Böhler, the Moravian. It was Böhler who, under God, was to sow the seeds of Charles Wesley's conversion on Whitsunday 1738. For some twenty years Charles travelled incessantly as a 'field preacher' and pastor of the growing Society of Methodism, based for many years in Bristol and finally settling in London in his middle sixties.

He has been described as 'a simple man . . . an ordinary man, although endowed with a gift of verse, the greatest single gift which either brother possessed'. The earliest biographer of John Wesley was the author John Hampson. Writing in 1791, he gives this picture of Charles:

> This gentleman was of a warm and lively disposition, of great frankness and integrity, and there was a warmness in his nature which some would perhaps call precipitancy and imprudence. He had a great regard for men of principle in all persuasions, and with all his heart abhorred a hypocrite. His conversation was pleasing and instructive and often seasoned with wit and humour. His religion was of the right sort: not gloomy and cynical, but cheerful and benevolent.

J. E. Rattenbury, to whom I owe the quotation above, adds: 'He seems to have been an English gentleman, without subtlety, untrained in casuistry, but of great family affection, with loyalties, especially to his brother, of the most attractive and enduring character.' There will be other glimpses in the pages that follow, to reveal his energy, his courage, his compassion, and above all his spiritual vitality and the warmth of his devotion. The *Dictionary of National Biography* gives this sketch of him in old age: 'He was of low stature but not slight, near-sighted, and abrupt and even odd in manner. Always absent-minded, he could read and compose at his ease, oblivious of his company.' Without that last endowment he could hardly have become 'the most gifted and indefatigable hymn-writer that England has ever known'.

He was distressed by the growing gulf between the Society and the Church of England. When in 1784, in a private room after a religious service, John Wesley laid hands on Dr Thomas Coke (already a duly ordained priest of the Church of England) for work among the fifteen thousand American Methodists, including the ordaining of his assistant, Charles expressed his mind in a number of satirical and biting verses:

> So easily are Bishops made
>   By man's, or woman's whim?
> W— his hands on C— has laid,
>   But who laid hands on him?

At the end, Charles declared to his own local vicar: 'Sir, whatever the world may have thought of me, I have lived and die a communicant of the Church of England, and I wish to be buried in the yard of my parish church.'

And so indeed he was.

In selecting the 138 poems that follow I have been conscious of how small a part they represent of Charles Wesley's writing, or even of his published work. Room has been found however for a fair sprinkling of his better known poems; including of course a number which appear in contemporary hymnals or from which current hymns have been extracted. Where this has happened the Index (on page 157) gives both the first line of the hymn and the first line of the whole poem. For the rest, I have sought *variety*, not only of theme, but of metre, mood and – to some extent – date of authorship. I make no claim, therefore, that this selection could be called 'the cream of Charles Wesley'; for though it includes some *tours de force* there are also a number of much more modest – and in a few instances, even pedestrian – items which while less familiar are not unrepresentative of his enormous output, and have a charm of their own. There is a considerable body of his verse which bears very little spiritual content or none at all; but since part of my purpose is to offer a devotional anthology in a small compass I have not found room for this or for his more polemical poems. Indeed length has been a difficulty; I determined at the outset to print each item in full so that his work may be seen complete as he wrote it; and this has had the effect of making it impossible to include a number of his longer poems.

Most people who know anything of Charles Wesley's work know it from their hymn book. It may come as a surprise to some to discover that while in certain instances (for example *119* and *121*) the hymn we sing today is the text Charles Wesley wrote, in others (see, for example *4* or *66*) the hymn has been carved out of the original text as a statue from the rock. 'Soldiers of Christ, arise' (*94*) has I think never appeared in full as a hymn – for obvious reasons. John Wesley, in his 1780 *A Collection of Hymns for the use of the People called Methodists*, included twelve of the sixteen verses, divided into three separate hymns. *Hymns and Psalms*, the latest Methodist hymnbook (1983) includes seven verses, making two hymns of them. Only, so far as I know, in the *New Oxford Book of Christian Verse (1981)* is the whole readily to hand. General anthologies are almost bound to select and abbreviate: even Lord David Cecil on editing his earlier *Oxford Book of Christian Verse* (1948) omitted one verse of 'Wrestling Jacob'.

There is a continuing discussion over the authorship of a number of the Wesley hymns. Ways have been suggested by which to determine whether the author of a given text was John or Charles; but the criteria themselves have never been agreed. *Hymns and Psalms* therefore adds to its list of 166 hymns attributed to Charles a note saying that the authorship of eight of them is in dispute and that their Index of Contributors should not be taken as a final word on the issue. A very few of the following verses *may* therefore be by John rather than by Charles (*10* and *49* would be the most significant); but since the brothers were themselves generally unconcerned to assert the distinction it would be wrong to make too much of it here. It is my own view that Charles demonstrated a remarkable humility of authorship (a notoriously difficult area in which to practise it) by permitting or encouraging publication of much of his best work under an undifferentiated common authorship; and by allowing John the editorial freedom revealed in comparing the *Collection* of 1780 with Charles's originals. It was once said by Virginia Woolf that the judgement of contemporaries in matters of poetry is almost always wrong; she cites how most of Christina Rossetti's complete works were rejected by her editors and adds, 'Her annual income from her poetry was for many years about ten pounds.' I do not know whether Charles earned even that amount as income from his verse; but of John Wesley's editorial abilities there can be no question. Dr Henry Bett writes:

> It is only when you go through the original volumes of Charles Wesley's verse, and note the way in which his brother chose the best of the hymns, and then omitted from these the weaker stanzas, until out of a long string of verses of very varied quality there often emerges a hymn of sustained excellence, which is a complete lyric in itself – it is only after such a study that one realizes the excellence of John Wesley's editorial work.

The pattern I have adopted is designed to draw together poems written at different dates and in different circumstances into a common theme. It is of course a very arbitrary choice;

and a given hymn could often appear equally well under some other heading – *29*, for example, on the Lord's Supper could have been included under chapter 4. I hope, however, that this arrangement will serve to break the body of the text into more manageable portions; and to allow some further background material to be included where it becomes relevant, without adding to the length of this Introduction.

John's editorial powers were exercised over the theology as well as over length, selection and presentation. We see this in *20*, which shows that Charles wrote in verse two, 'Take away our *power* of sinning', suggesting a view of Christian perfection which John censured in his *Collection* by the omission of this verse (it is sometimes used today with a change suggested by John Fletcher of Madeley, 'Take away the *love* of sinning'). Dr Bett gives several instances of John's marginal annotations criticizing Charles's theology. Against the line 'Thou didst in love Thy servant leave', John writes 'Never. – J.W.'; against 'And all our rapturous happiness/In hasty sorrow ends', he writes 'Not always. – J.W.' But though John was ready to criticize and edit his brother's wor , he made clear in the famous Preface to the 1780 *Collection* that this was not a liberty allowed to others. What would he have made, I wonder, of those later editors who used what Bernard Lord Manning called 'a literary Keating's Powder: a sort of spiritual insect killer – fatal to worms'? Manning applied this vivid metaphor to the general loss of nerve that would water down strong spiritual expressions in hymnody; of which he took the description of human beings as 'worms' as a typical example. Certainly it is a word regularly found in Charles Wesley's verse, though I have tried to limit the number of times it appears in this selection; as indeed I have with the word 'bowels'. When it was generally thought that the organs of the body were responsible for various emotions, the bowels (since the sixteenth century the interior of anything – compare the bowels of the earth) were thought to govern pity – hence 'bowels of compassion'. It is not

Wesley's fault that the word has come since his day to have a less general and more specific meaning.

Again, Charles Wesley, as will be seen, had a high regard for the proper use of rhyme. Broadly speaking, we scarcely find in his work a pair of lines which could, within the metre, carry a rhyme and yet do not do so. Certainly he can be very free in the approximations of his rhyme, letting the strong flow of language carry the hymn forward. He rhymes nature/ creator, compassion/salvation, venture/enter, and so on. He cheerfully employs a rhyme which today would be thought only suitable for comic verse, writing:

> Some put their trust in chariots,
>   And horses some rely on,
>   But Christ alone
>   His people own
> The health and strength of Zion.

But it should be remembered that since his day some words have changed their pronunciation and so wrecked what, when he wrote it, was an impeccable rhyme. *Join* is the classic example, which (as can be amply demonstrated from other writers) was then pronounced *jine* and so rhymed with *thine* or with *divine*. G. H. Vallins in *The Wesleys and the English Language* has carefully analysed the 'imperfect' rhymes of Charles Wesley; and though I find some of his defence spirited rather than convincing, his six classifications deserve study before we assume that a particular couplet represents careless or hasty workmanship. Dr Bett and Dr Frank Baker both offer lists of words where time has changed the pronunciation and so disturbed what was originally a perfect rhyme – words such as *convert*, which in Wesley's day rhymed with *art*; or *great* which is sometimes used to rhyme with *feet*. In metre, too, it should be noted that *Spirit* was in Wesley's time acceptable as a mono- syllable – *Sprit* (compare our word 'sprite'); and is so used, for example, in *52* and on several other occasions. Other words have changed their pronunciation and metrical stress – for example 'as*cert*ained' (compare *4*) or '*ac*ceptable' (compare *121*, where today's hymnals substitute 'And prove Thy good and perfect will').

The text I have followed throughout is that of Dr G. Osborn, in his monumental *The Poetical Works of John and Charles Wesley* (thirteen volumes, Wesleyan Methodist Conference Office, London 1868–72). His edition includes the last corrections of the authors; and modernizes a certain amount of spelling, capitalization and the use of italics. The one manuscript poem (*97*) not in Dr Osborn's collection, is taken from Dr Baker's *Representative Verse of Charles Wesley*. I have carried a little further Dr Osborn's editorial revisions of the matters mentioned above, though no word of the text has been changed. Indeed, a number of capital letters have been retained which might be out of place in contemporary verse, including personifications and pronouns of deity, the beginning of every line, and the internal capital when Charles Wesley compressed two lines of verse into one line of type, as in *70*. Titles of the hymns, where they appear, are almost always either taken from the original or supplied from within the poem: exceptions are *134* and *138*. Texts of Scripture appearing above a hymn are those set there by the author; but sometimes abbreviated. Where a text is self-evident or appears to add nothing, I have felt free to omit it. I owe a debt to those who have made it possible for me to prepare this small anthology. As always, the University Library at Cambridge have been unfailingly helpful (though lacking the last two volumes of Dr Osborn's set, should any benefactor have them to donate). The authorities of Wesley House, Cambridge, generously allowed me the use of their library; and Dr David Keep, Senior Lecturer in the Faculty of Arts and Social Sciences at Rolle College, Exmouth, enabled me to acquire Dr Osborn's volumes for myself. No writer on Wesley's hymns can escape a vast obligation to Dr Frank Baker for his definitive study, *Representative Verse of Charles Wesley* (Epworth 1962), now quite unobtainable; but in my case the obligation was compounded by the gift from Dr Baker, through Professor S. Paul Schilling, of a copy of his *Charles Wesley's Verse: an Introduction* (Epworth 1964), the invaluable introductory material from his larger work. I am very grateful, too, to the editor of Triangle Books, SPCK, for suggesting this present book to me and for its publication.

Besides Dr Frank Baker, no one has written more perceptively on Charles Wesley than Dr Henry Bett in his *Hymns of Methodism* (enlarged edition, Epworth 1945) or more persuasively than Bernard Lord Manning in his *The Hymns of Wesley and Watts* (Epworth 1942). John Telford in his day, and more recently J. E. Rattenbury, wrote much about Charles Wesley and are invaluable guides. He is also the subject of a distinguished chapter, contributed by William F. Lofthouse, in volume one of *A History of the Methodist Church in Great Britain* (Epworth 1965). R. Newton Flew published his *The Hymns of Charles Wesley: a study of their structure* (Epworth) in 1953, George H. Findlay his study of the hymns entitled *Christ's Standard Bearer* (Epworth) in 1956, and George H. Vallins his *The Wesleys and the English Language* (Epworth) in 1957. The most recent selection known to me is that of David and Jill Wright with their admirable *Thirty Hymns of the Wesleys* (Paternoster Press) in 1985. Other collections (now mainly out of print) include *Wesley's Prayers and Praises* by J. Alan Kay (Epworth 1958), *The Richest Legacy: eucharistic hymns of John and Charles Wesley* by J. R. Burton (no date; privately printed), *A Rapture of Praise* by H. A. Hodges and A. M. Allchin (Hodder & Stoughton 1966), and the volume *John and Charles Wesley: selected writings and hymns* (SPCK 1981) in the series 'The Classics of Western Spirituality'. The Horton Trust of Bradford published *Hymns of Eternal Truth* (120 poems of the Wesley brothers) in 1971; and in America the Lillenas Publishing Company issued *Wesley Hymns* (1982) complete with music, compiled by Ken Bible and containing 164 items. Lillenas had earlier (1963) published the *Wesley Hymnbook* with 154 hymns. The theology of the hymns has been treated most recently in *A Thousand Tongues* by John Lawson (Paternoster Press, Exeter 1987) subtitled 'The Wesley hymns as a guide to scriptural teaching'. This present book contains items which are not included in any of these.

A select bibliography will be found in Dr Baker's *Charles Wesley's Verse* and in the monumental Oxford Edition of the Works of John Wesley, volume seven, consisting of a new critical edition of *A Collection of Hymns for the use of the People called Methodists* (Clarendon Press, Oxford 1983).

To my many Methodist friends, as we approach the bicentenary, with much diffidence I offer this little book.

Ruan Minor, 1986.   T.D.S.

1 Christ in Experience

Conversion to Christ · The eternal Son · Christ our Redeemer
Christ our Advocate · Christ our King · Christ in the heart

John Wesley's celebrated account of his conversion to Christ, taken from his journal of May 1738, is widely known. 'What occurred on Wednesday the 24th, I think best to relate at large,' he begins, and in fourteen numbered paragraphs he recounts his baptism and schooldays, his early spiritual experiences, his ordination and ministry both at home and in Savannah, and his search for peace. 'In this vile, abject state of bondage to sin, I was indeed fighting continually,' he says, 'but not conquering.' He describes how, in the evening of 24 May, 'I went very unwillingly to a society in Aldersgate-street, where one was reading Luther's preface to the Epistle to the Romans. About a quarter before nine, while he was describing the change which God works in the heart through faith in Christ, I felt my heart strangely warmed. I felt I did trust in Christ, Christ alone, for salvation; and an assurance was given me, that he had taken away *my* sins, even *mine*, and saved *me* from the law of sin and death.'

What is less well known is that Charles had won his way to just such a saving faith three days earlier, on Whitsunday 1738, in the home of 'a poor ignorant mechanic' called Bray. Unwell, and much in prayer, he heard a voice saying 'In the name of Jesus of Nazareth, arise, and believe, and thou shalt be healed of all thy infirmities.' It was in fact the voice of Mr Bray's sister, who had felt herself commanded in a dream to say these words. Charles got out of bed and opening his Bible read from the Psalms: 'He hath put a new song in my mouth, even praise unto our God,' followed by the first verse of Isaiah 40, 'Comfort ye, comfort ye my people, saith your God.' He wrote in his journal, 'I now found myself at peace with God, and rejoiced in the hope of loving Christ.'

[1]

Two days later he began a hymn upon his conversion; but broke off, for fear of pride. He was encouraged to continue, finished the hymn, and sang it next day in company with his brother who had been brought from Aldersgate Street 'by a troop of our friends' declaring 'I believe'. The hymn, almost certainly, was 'Where shall my wondering soul begin'.

Some of the most celebrated of all Charles Wesley's hymns appear in this first section. 'Free Grace' (2), has been sung continually from its first publication in 1739 (though usually omitting verse five). 'Wrestling Jacob', drawn from the story of Jacob wrestling with the angel in Genesis 32, was said by Isaac Watts 'to be worth all the verses he himself had written'.

But it is right to look first at 'Where shall my wondering soul begin'. J. E. Rattenbury, the Methodist scholar, describes vividly the scene of its first singing, in his critical study *The Conversion of the Wesleys*:

> No more strangely prophetic verses were ever written. How should this little sick man imagine as he seems to have done, the men and women to whom he and his brother will in the future appeal? What likelihood that the voices of these High Anglicans should ever reach such people? No one yet had even imagined field preaching. That sick room must have been crowded with ghosts of the future as Charles Wesley penned the prelude to the great revival. Nothing in Methodist history is more appealing than the vision of those two little men, with streaming but joyous faces, singing in a sick room their evangelical duet . . .

Conversion to Christ

1

CHRIST THE FRIEND OF SINNERS

Where shall my wondering soul begin?
　　How shall I all to heaven aspire?
A slave redeemed from death and sin,
　　A brand plucked from eternal fire,
How shall I equal triumphs raise,
And sing my great Deliverer's praise!

O, how shall I the goodness tell,
　　Father, which Thou to me hast showed?
That I, a child of wrath and hell,
　　I should be called a child of God!
Should know, should feel my sins forgiven,
Blest with this antepast of heaven!

And shall I slight my Father's love,
　　Or basely fear His gifts to own?
Unmindful of His favours prove?
　　Shall I, the hallowed cross to shun,
Refuse His righteousness t' impart,
By hiding it within my heart?

No – though the ancient dragon rage,
　　And call forth all his hosts to war;
Though earth's self-righteous sons engage;
　　Them, and their god, alike I dare:
Jesus, the sinner's Friend, proclaim;
Jesus, to sinners still the same.

Outcasts of men, to you I call,
   Harlots, and publicans, and thieves!
He spreads His arms t' embrace you all;
   Sinners alone His grace receives:
No need of Him the righteous have,
He came the lost to seek and save.

Come, all ye Magdalens in lust,
   Ye ruffians fell in murders old;
Repent, and live: despair and trust!
   Jesus for you to death was sold;
Though hell protest, and earth repine,
He died for crimes like yours – and mine.

Come, O my guilty brethren, come,
   Groaning beneath your load of sin!
His bleeding heart shall make you room,
   His open side shall take you in.
He calls you now, invites you home:
Come, O my guilty brethren, come!

For you the purple current flowed
   In pardons from His wounded side:
Languished for you th' eternal God,
   For you the Prince of Glory died.
Believe, and all your guilt's forgiven;
Only believe – and yours is heaven.

FREE GRACE

And can it be, that I should gain
    An interest in the Saviour's blood?
Died He for me? – who caused His pain!
    For me? – who Him to death pursued.
Amazing love! how can it be
That Thou, my God, shouldst die for me?

'Tis mystery all! th' Immortal dies!
    Who can explore His strange design?
In vain the first-born seraph tries
    To sound the depths of love divine.
'Tis mercy all! Let earth adore;
Let angel minds inquire no more.

He left His Father's throne above,
    (So free, so infinite His grace!)
Emptied Himself of all but love,
    And bled for Adam's helpless race:
'Tis mercy all, immense and free!
For, O my God! it found out me!

Long my imprisoned spirit lay,
    Fast bound in sin and nature's night:
Thine eye diffused a quickening ray;
    I woke; the dungeon flamed with light;
My chains fell off, my heart was free,
I rose, went forth, and followed Thee.

Still the small inward voice I hear,
    That whispers all my sins forgiven;
Still the atoning blood is near,
    That quenched the wrath of hostile heaven:
I feel the life His wounds impart;
I feel my Saviour in my heart.

No condemnation now I dread,
    Jesus, and all in Him, is mine:
Alive in Him, my living Head,
    And clothed in righteousness divine,
Bold I approach th' eternal throne,
And claim the crown, through Christ, my own.

3

WRESTLING JACOB

Come, O Thou Traveller unknown,
    Whom still I hold, but cannot see,
My company before is gone,
    And I am left alone with Thee;
With Thee all night I mean to stay,
And wrestle till the break of day.

I need not tell Thee who I am,
    My misery or sin declare,
Thyself hast called me by my name,
    Look on Thy hands, and read it there;
But who, I ask Thee, who art Thou?
Tell me Thy name, and tell me now.

In vain Thou strugglest to get free,
  I never will unloose my hold;
Art thou the Man that died for me?
  The secret of Thy love unfold;
Wrestling I will not let Thee go
Till I Thy name, Thy nature know.

Wilt Thou not yet to me reveal
  Thy new, unutterable name?
Tell me, I still beseech Thee, tell;
  To know it now resolved I am;
Wrestling I will not let Thee go
Till I Thy name, Thy nature know.

'Tis all in vain to hold Thy tongue,
  Or touch the hollow of my thigh;
Though every sinew be unstrung,
  Out of my arms Thou shalt not fly;
Wrestling I will not let Thee go
Till I Thy name, Thy nature know.

What though my shrinking flesh complain,
  And murmur to contend so long,
I rise superior to my pain,
  When I am weak then I am strong;
And when my all of strength shall fail,
I shall with the God-man prevail.

My strength is gone, my nature dies,
  I sink beneath Thy weighty hand,
Faint to revive, and fall to rise;
  I fall, and yet by faith I stand,
I stand, and will not let Thee go,
Till I Thy name, Thy nature know.

Yield to me now; for I am weak,
    But confident in self-despair:
Speak to my heart, in blessings speak,
    Be conquered by my instant prayer;
Speak, or Thou never hence shalt move,
And tell me if Thy name is Love.

'Tis Love! 'tis Love! Thou diedst for me;
    I hear Thy whisper in my heart:
The morning breaks, the shadows flee:
    Pure universal Love Thou art;
To me, to all Thy bowels move;
Thy nature, and Thy name is Love.

My prayer hath power with God; the grace
    Unspeakable I now receive,
Through faith I see Thee face to face;
    I see Thee face to face, and live:
In vain I have not wept and strove;
Thy nature, and Thy name is Love.

I know Thee, Saviour, who Thou art,
    Jesus, the feeble sinner's Friend;
Nor wilt Thou with the night depart,
    But stay, and love me to the end;
Thy mercies never shall remove;
Thy nature, and Thy name is Love.

The Sun of Righteousness on me
    Hath rose with healing in His wings;
Withered my nature's strength, from Thee
    My soul its life and succour brings;
My help is all laid up above;
Thy nature, and Thy name is Love.

Contented now upon my thigh
   I halt, till life's short journey end;
All helplessness, all weakness, I
   On Thee alone for strength depend,
Nor have I power from Thee to move;
Thy nature, and Thy name is Love.

Lame as I am, I take the prey,
   Hell, earth, and sin with ease o'ercome;
I leap for joy, pursue my way,
   And as a bounding hart fly home,
Through all eternity to prove,
Thy nature, and Thy name is Love.

4

FOR THE ANNIVERSARY DAY OF ONE'S CONVERSION

Glory to God, and praise, and love
   Be ever, ever given,
By saints below, and saints above,
   The church in earth and heaven.

On this glad day the glorious Sun
   Of Righteousness arose;
On my benighted soul He shone,
   And filled it with repose.

Sudden expired the legal strife;
   'Twas then I ceased to grieve;
My second, real, living life
   I then began to live.

Then with my heart I first believed,
    Believed with faith divine;
Power with the Holy Ghost received
    To call the Saviour mine.

I felt my Lord's atoning blood
    Close to *my* soul applied;
Me, me He loved – the Son of God
    For *me*, for *me* He died!

I found, and owned His promise true,
    Ascertained of my part;
My pardon passed in heaven I knew,
    When written on my heart.

O for a thousand tongues to sing
    My dear Redeemer's praise!
The glories of my God and King,
    The triumphs of His grace.

My gracious Master, and my God,
    Assist me to proclaim,
To spread through all the earth abroad
    The honours of Thy name.

Jesus, the name that charms our fears,
    That bids our sorrows cease;
'Tis music in the sinner's ears,
    'Tis life, and health, and peace!

He breaks the power of cancelled sin,
    He sets the prisoner free;
His blood can make the foulest clean,
    His blood availed for me.

He speaks; and, listening to His voice,
  New life the dead receive,
The mournful, broken hearts rejoice,
  The humble poor believe.

Hear Him, ye deaf; His praise, ye dumb,
  Your loosened tongues employ;
Ye blind, behold your Saviour come;
  And leap, ye lame, for joy.

Look unto Him, ye nations; own
  Your God, ye fallen race!
Look, and be saved through faith alone;
  Be justified by grace!

See all your sins on Jesus laid;
  The Lamb of God was slain,
His soul was once an offering made
  For every soul of man.

Harlots, and publicans, and thieves
  In holy triumph join;
Saved is the sinner that believes
  From crimes as great as mine.

Murderers, and all ye hellish crew,
  Ye sons of lust and pride,
Believe the Saviour died for you;
  For me the Saviour died.

Awake from guilty nature's sleep,
  And Christ shall give you light,
Cast all your sins into the deep,
  And wash the Ethiop white.

With me, your chief, you then shall know,
  Shall feel your sins forgiven;
Anticipate your heaven below,
  And own that love is heaven.

5

Stupendous love of God most high!
He comes to meet us from the sky
    In mildest majesty,
Full of unutterable grace
He calls the weary burdened race,
    Come all for help to Me.

Tired with the greatness of my way,
From Him I would no longer stray,
    But rest in Jesus have,
Weary of sin, from sin would cease,
Weary of mine own righteousness,
    And stoop myself to save.

Weary of passions unsubdued,
Weary of vows in vain renewed,
    Of forms without the power,
Of prayers, and hopes, complaints, and groans,
My fainting soul in silence owns
    I can hold out no more.

Beneath this mountain-load of grief,
Of guilt and desperate unbelief,
    Jesus, Thy creature see,
With all my nature's weight oppressed,
I sink, I die, for want of rest,
    Yet cannot come to Thee.

Mine utter helplessness I feel;
But Thou, who gav'st the feeble will,
    Th' effectual grace supply:
Be Thou my strength, my light, my way,
And bid my soul the call obey,
    And to Thy bosom fly.

Fulfil Thine own intense desire,
And now into my heart inspire
    The power of faith and love;
Then Saviour, then to Thee I come,
And find on earth the life, the home,
    The rest of saints above.

The eternal Son

6

What think ye of Christ?   Matthew 22.42

I think Him David's Son
    Whom David Lord doth call:
I think Him God and man in one,
    I think Him all in all.

I think Him the Most High,
    Sole, self-existing God,
Made flesh, a sinful world to buy,
    And save us through His blood.

I think Him perfect Love
    Who groaned on Calvary:
I more than think His bowels move
    To such a worm as me.

I think Him still the same,
　　My Ransomer divine;
I think if His through life I am
　　He is for ever mine.

7

The Word was God   John 1.1

The Word was independent God,
　　God uncreated and supreme:
All things from Him their Fountain flowed,
　　Whate'er was made, was made by Him:
When heaven and earth began to be,
　　The glorious absolute I AM,
He was from all eternity
　　To all eternity the same.

8

The voice of God the Father sounds
　　Salvation to our sinful race:
His grace above our sin abounds,
　　His glory shines in Jesus' face,
And by the person of the Son
The Father makes salvation known.

Saved by the Son, the Lord our God
　　Jehovah's Fellow we proclaim,
Who washes us in His own blood,
　　To us declares His Father's name,
His nature pure, His love imparts,
With all His fulness to our hearts.

The end of sin and death is near:
  The Man shall then to God resign
His kingdom and dominion here,
  His exercise of grace divine,
The kingdom which His Father gave,
The delegated power to save.

When all His friends are saved at last,
  And all His enemies destroyed,
The Mediator's sway is past,
  His office and commission void,
The Man's authority is o'er,
And Christ for sinners pleads no more.

But Christ the God maintains His throne,
  No period shall His kingdom see,
By nature with His Father one,
  A King from all eternity,
The same Jehovah He remains,
And o'er His saints for ever reigns.

10

IN AFFLICTION

Eternal Beam of light divine,
  Fountain of unexhausted love,
In whom the Father's glories shine,
  Through earth beneath, and heaven above!

Jesu! the weary wanderer's rest;
　　Give me Thy easy yoke to bear,
With steadfast patience arm my breast,
　　With spotless love and lowly fear.

Thankful I take the cup from Thee,
　　Prepared and mingled by Thy skill;
Though bitter to the taste it be,
　　Powerful the wounded soul to heal.

Be Thou, O Rock of Ages, nigh:
　　So shall each murmuring thought be gone,
And grief, and fear, and care shall fly,
　　As clouds before the midday sun.

Speak to my warring passions, 'Peace;'
　　Say to my trembling heart, 'Be still:'
Thy power my strength and fortress is,
　　For all things serve Thy sovereign will.

O death, where is thy sting? where now
　　Thy boasted victory, O grave?
Who shall contend with God; or who
　　Can hurt whom God delights to save?

Christ our Redeemer

11

With glorious clouds encompassed round
　　Whom angels dimly see,
Will the Unsearchable be found,
　　Or God appear to me?

Will He forsake His throne above,
　　Himself to worms impart?
Answer Thou Man of grief and love,
　　And speak into my heart.

In manifested love explain
　　Thy wonderful design,
What meant the suffering Son of man,
　　The streaming blood divine?

Didst Thou not in our flesh appear,
　　And live and die below,
That I may now perceive Thee near,
　　And my Redeemer know?

Come then, and to my soul reveal
　　The heights and depths of grace,
Those wounds which all my sorrows heal,
　　That dear disfigured face.

Before my eyes of faith confessed
　　Stand forth a slaughtered Lamb,
And wrap me in Thy crimson vest,
　　And tell me all Thy name.

Jehovah in Thy person show,
　　Jehovah crucified,
And then the pardoning God I know,
　　And feel the blood applied;

I view the Lamb in His own light
　　Whom angels dimly see,
And gaze transported at the sight
　　Through all eternity.

Who is a God like unto thee, that pardoneth . . . ? Micah 7.18

Jesus, who is a God like Thee!
   The God of pardoning grace
Will not impute iniquity
   To the believing race:
He passes all our follies by,
   And all our sins forgives,
His wrath doth in a moment die,
   His love for ever lives.

13

Who God in Christ discover
   By His own Spirit's power,
And love our heavenly Lover,
   And One in Three adore,
The secret hid from ages,
   Having our Saviour's mind,
We in the sacred pages
   And we alone can find.

Assenting to the letter
   A sinner nothing gains:
It cannot free the debtor,
   Or break the prisoner's chains;
The truest, soundest notion
   Can never guilt remove,
Or give that heart-devotion
   Which flows from humble love.

Thou God who sin forgivest,
    To Thee if sinners turn,
And in Thine arms receivest
    When after Thee we mourn;
Thy gospel's controversy
    Against the men maintain
Who spurn Thy pardoning mercy,
    And bear Thy name in vain.

The world of misbelievers
    Thou only canst convince,
Orthodox self-deceivers
    Shut up in all their sins:
Darkness for light mistaking
    And light for darkness, they
O'erlook the one thing lacking,
    Or scornfully gainsay.

Our faith, imagination,
    Our hope they count a lie,
The present, sure salvation,
    The heartfelt love deny;
The witness of that Spirit,
    The antepast, and seal,
And His imputed merit
    Who saves us all from hell.

Their shadowy faith embracing,
    A creature of their own,
Thee with their sins confessing
    They bow to three in one;
Assured they only know Thee,
    With sin they will not part,
Or render that they owe Thee,
    An undivided heart.

Stir up Thy saving power,
    Mysterious One in Three,
Nor let the pit devour
    The souls redeemed by Thee:
Convince of their delusion
    The enemies of grace,
And clothe them with confusion,
    That they may seek Thy face.

Beneath their burden groaning
    When after Thee they cry,
Their unbelief bemoaning
    As at the point to die,
From guilt and condemnation
    Thy penitents to clear,
The God of their salvation,
    The Triune God appear.

14

Today shalt thou be with me in paradise.   Luke 23.43

A monument of mercy's power,
    Rescued by Jesus on the tree,
Saved at the last tremendous hour
    One soul, and only one we see,
With brokenness of heart sincere
That all may hope, that all may fear.

He but to be remembered wants,
    The time and all things else he leaves:
More than he asks the Saviour grants,
    A kingdom promises and gives,
'I will My majesty display,
And thou shalt reign with Me to-day.'

15

What doth the ladder mean,
Sent down from the Most High?
Fastened to earth its foot is seen,
Its summit to the sky:
Lo! up and down the scale
The angels swiftly move,
And God, the great Invisible,
Himself appears above!

Jesus that ladder is,
Th' incarnate Deity,
Partaker of celestial bliss
And human misery;
Sent from His high abode,
To sleeping mortals given,
He stands, and man unites to God,
And earth connects with heaven.

Christ our Advocate

16

Father, if I have sinned, with Thee
An Advocate I have:
Jesus, the Just, shall plead for me;
The sinner Christ shall save.

Pardon and peace in Him I find:
    But not for me alone
The Lamb was slain; for all mankind
    His blood did once atone.

My soul is on Thy promise cast,
    And lo! I claim my part:
The universal pardon's past;
    O seal it on my heart.

Thou canst not now Thy grace deny;
    Thou canst not but forgive;
Lord, if Thy justice asks me why –
    In Jesus I believe!

Christ our King

17

Jesu, my God and King,
    Thy regal state I sing.
Thou, and only Thou art great,
    High Thine everlasting throne;
Thou the sovereign Potentate,
    Blest, immortal Thou alone.

Essay your choicest strains,
    The King Messiah reigns!
Tune your harps, celestial choir,
    Joyful all, your voices raise,
Christ, than earth-born monarchs higher,
    Sons of men and angels, praise.

Hail your dread Lord and ours,
  Dominions, thrones, and powers!
Source of power, He rules alone:
  Veil your eyes, and prostrate fall,
Cast your crowns before His throne,
  Hail the Cause, the Lord of all!

Let earth's remotest bound
  With echoing joys resound;
Christ to praise let all conspire:
  Praise doth all to Christ belong;
Shout, ye first-born sons of fire;
  Earth, repeat the glorious song.

Worthy, O Lord, art Thou
  That every knee should bow,
Every tongue to Thee confess,
  Universal nature join
Strong and mighty Thee to bless,
  Gracious, merciful, benign!

Wisdom is due to Thee,
  And might and majesty:
Thee in mercy rich we prove;
  Glory, honour, praise receive;
Worthy Thou of all our love,
  More than all we pant to give.

Justice and truth maintain
  Thy everlasting reign.
One with Thine almighty Sire,
  Partner of an equal throne,
King of hearts, let all conspire
  Gratefully Thy sway to own.

Prince of the hosts of God,
    Display Thy power abroad:
Strong and high is Thy right hand,
    Terrible in majesty!
Who can in Thine anger stand?
    Who the vengeful bolt can flee?

    Thee when the dragon's pride
        To battle vain defied,
Brighter than the morning star,
    Lucifer as lightning fell,
For from heaven, from glory far,
    Headlong hurled to deepest hell.

    Sin felt of old Thy power,
        Thou patient Conqueror!
Long he vexed the world below,
    Long they groaned beneath his reign;
Thou destroy'dst the tyrant foe,
    Thou redeem'dst the captive, man.

    Trembles the King of Fears
        Whene'er Thy cross appears.
Once its dreadful force he found:
    Saviour, cleave again the sky;
Slain by an eternal wound,
    Death shall then for ever die!

Rejoice, the Lord is King!
    Your Lord and King adore,
Mortals, give thanks, and sing,
    And triumph evermore:
Lift up your heart, lift up your voice,
Rejoice, again I say, rejoice.

Jesus the Saviour reigns,
    The God of truth and love,
When He had purged our stains,
    He took His seat above:
Lift up your heart, lift up your voice,
Rejoice, again I say, rejoice.

His kingdom cannot fail,
    He rules o'er earth and heaven,
The keys of death and hell
    Are to our Jesus given:
Lift up your heart, lift up your voice,
Rejoice, again I say, rejoice.

He sits at God's right hand,
    Till all His foes submit,
And bow to His command,
    And fall beneath His feet:
Lift up your heart, lift up your voice,
Rejoice, again I say, rejoice.

He all His foes shall quell,
   Shall all our sins destroy,
And every bosom swell
   With pure seraphic joy:
Lift up your heart, lift up your voice,
Rejoice, again I say, rejoice.

Rejoice in glorious hope,
   Jesus the Judge shall come;
And take His servants up
   To their eternal home:
We soon shall hear th' archangel's voice,
The trump of God shall sound, Rejoice.

Christ in the heart

19

Thou hidden Source of calm repose,
   Thou all-sufficient Love divine,
My Help, and Refuge from my foes,
   Secure I am, if Thou art mine,
And lo! from sin, and grief, and shame
I hide me, Jesus, in Thy name.

Thy mighty name salvation is,
   And keeps my happy soul above;
Comfort it brings, and power, and peace,
   And joy, and everlasting love:
To me with Thy dear name are given
Pardon, and holiness, and heaven.

Jesu, my all in all Thou art,
   My rest in toil, my ease in pain,
The medicine of my broken heart,
   In war my peace, in loss my gain,
My smile beneath the tyrant's frown,
In shame my glory, and my crown.

In want my plentiful supply,
   In weakness my almighty power,
In bonds my perfect liberty,
   My light in Satan's darkest hour,
In grief my joy unspeakable,
My life in death, my heaven in hell.

20

Love divine, all loves excelling,
   Joy of heaven, to earth come down,
Fix in us Thy humble dwelling,
   All Thy faithful mercies crown:
Jesu, Thou art all compassion,
   Pure, unbounded love Thou art,
Visit us with Thy salvation,
   Enter every trembling heart.

Breathe, O breathe Thy loving Spirit,
   Into every troubled breast,
Let us all in Thee inherit,
   Let us find that second rest:
Take away our power of sinning,
   Alpha and Omega be,
End of faith as its beginning,
   Set our hearts at liberty.

Come, almighty to deliver,
   Let us all Thy life receive;
Suddenly return, and never,
   Never more Thy temples leave.
Thee we would be always blessing,
   Serve Thee as Thy hosts above,
Pray, and praise Thee without ceasing,
   Glory in Thy perfect love.

Finish then Thy new creation,
   Pure, and spotless let us be,
Let us see Thy great salvation,
   Perfectly restored in Thee:
Changed from glory into glory,
   Till in heaven we take our place,
Till we cast our crowns before Thee,
   Lost in wonder, love, and praise!

2 The Christian Year

Advent · Christmas · The New Year · The Transfiguration
The Entry into Jerusalem · The Upper Room · Passiontide · Easter
Ascension · Pentecost · Trinity · The Meeting of Friends

When in 1780 John Wesley published his long-awaited hymn-book, *A Collection of Hymns for the use of the People called Methodists* ('Price Three Shillings, sewed'), he wrote in the Preface that he had made it 'large enough to contain all the important truths of our most holy religion ... in a regular order. The hymns are not carelessly jumbled together, but carefully ranged under proper heads, according to the experience of real Christians. So that this book is in effect a little body of experimental and practical divinity.'

Both John and Charles were, of course, clergymen of the Church of England, well accustomed to following in their Prayer Books the seasons of the Christian year. As can be glimpsed in the pages that follow, Charles wrote (as any hymn writer must) of these great events in hymn after hymn. But since that first Methodist hymn book was conceived to express experience, the arrangement owed nothing to seasonal use. Instead we have sections with such headings as 'Describing Heaven' (or Hell), 'Praying for a Blessing', 'Describing formal Religion', 'For Believers Rejoicing' (or Fighting, Praying, Suffering and so on), and 'For the Society'. It was designed as more of what today we should call a supplementary hymn book, rather than for the main daily and weekly worship of a parish or local church.

Nevertheless, Charles returned constantly to the great facts associated with Christmas, Holy Week, Easter, and the other seasons of the Church's year. In 1745 he issued a small collection of *Hymns on the Nativity of Our Lord* and a year later *Hymns for our Lord's Resurrection*, *Hymns for Ascension Day*, *Hymns to the Trinity* and *Hymns on the Great Festivals*.

High among his best known verses must be his 'Hymn for Christmas Day' (25). It forms a good example of how the work of editors as well as authors, and the judgement of the Church over a considerable period, combine to produce the final form of a great hymn. Though it appears here in full as Charles Wesley wrote it, it did not find its way into a hymn book for some fourteen years after its first publication. George Whitfield then included it in his collection, changing the opening lines to their present familiar form:

Hark! The herald angels sing
Glory to the new-born King!

and leaving out verses eight and ten. It did not appear in the Methodist book until 1831, and *Hymns Ancient and Modern* only began to use it in 1861. Their much-criticized 1904 edition unwisely returned to the opening lines in their original form. It was reported 'The public laughed long and loud: and it is hardly an exaggeration to say that "the welkin" gave the final death blow to the 1904 book.'

'Multiple authorship' is also illustrated in 'Lo! He comes with clouds descending' (21). In 1752 John Cennick, a former colleague of the Wesleys, published a hymn in this metre:

Lo! He cometh, countless trumpets
Blow before his bloody sign!

Wesley's appeared in 1758 in his *Hymns of Intercession for all Mankind*; while in 1760 Martin Madan, Chaplain of the Lock Hospital, issued a *Collection* in which parts of both of these were combined together to make a new version. The story is complicated still further by a very similar hymn of Thomas Olivers, and by various imitations, sometimes themselves embodying lines from Wesley's text!

'The Meeting of Friends' (46), is included here because by long tradition it is sung annually at the opening of the Methodist Conference.

21

Lo! He comes with clouds descending,
  Once for favoured sinners slain!
Thousand, thousand saints attending,
  Swell the triumph of His train:
    Hallelujah,
  God appears on earth to reign!

Every eye shall now behold Him
  Robed in dreadful majesty,
Those who set at nought and sold Him,
  Pierced, and nailed Him to the tree,
    Deeply wailing
  Shall the true Messiah see.

The dear tokens of His passion
  Still His dazzling body bears,
Cause of endless exultation
  To His ransomed worshippers;
    With what rapture
  Gaze we on those glorious scars!

Yea, Amen! let all adore Thee
  High on Thine eternal throne!
Saviour, take the power and glory,
  Claim the kingdom for Thine own,
    Jah, Jehovah,
  Everlasting God, come down.

Come, Thou long expected Jesus,
    Born to set Thy people free,
From our fears and sins release us,
    Let us find our rest in Thee:
Israel's strength and consolation,
    Hope of all the earth Thou art,
Dear Desire of every nation,
    Joy of every longing heart.

Born Thy people to deliver,
    Born a child and yet a king,
Born to reign in us for ever,
    Now Thy gracious kingdom bring:
By Thy own eternal Spirit
    Rule in all our hearts alone,
By Thy all-sufficient merit
    Raise us to Thy glorious throne.

Christmas

23

When He did our flesh assume,
    That everlasting Man,
Mary held Him in her womb
    Whom heaven could not contain!
Who the mystery can believe?
Incomprehensible Thou art:
    Yet we still by faith conceive,
    And bear Thee in our heart.

24

Let us now go even unto Bethlehem. Luke 2.15

Come, let us with speed To Bethlehem go,
The house of that bread Which God doth bestow:
To all He hath given And sent from above
The Banquet of Heaven, The Son of His love.

By faith we shall see Him promised of old,
And know it is He Of whom we were told;
That heavenly Stranger Fall prostrate before,
And God in a manger With angels adore.

25

HYMN FOR CHRISTMAS DAY

Hark how all the welkin rings,
'Glory to the King of kings,
Peace on earth, and mercy mild,
God and sinners reconciled!'

Joyful, all ye nations, rise,
Join the triumph of the skies;
Universal nature, say,
'Christ the Lord is born today!'

Christ, by highest heaven adored,
Christ, the everlasting Lord,
Late in time behold Him come,
Offspring of a virgin's womb.

Veiled in flesh, the Godhead see,
Hail th' incarnate Deity!
Pleased as man with men t' appear
Jesus, our Immanuel here!

Hail the heavenly Prince of Peace!
Hail the Sun of Righteousness!
Light and life to all He brings,
Risen with healing in His wings.

Mild He lays His glory by,
Born – that man no more may die,
Born – to raise the sons of earth,
Born – to give them second birth.

Come, Desire of Nations, come,
Fix in us Thy humble home;
Rise, the woman's conquering Seed,
Bruise in us the serpent's head.

Now display Thy saving power,
Ruined nature now restore;
Now in mystic union join
Thine to ours, and ours to Thine.

Adam's likeness, Lord, efface,
Stamp Thy image in its place;
Second Adam from above,
Reinstate us in Thy love.

Let us Thee, though lost, regain,
Thee, the Life, the Inner Man:
O! to all Thyself impart,
Formed in each believing heart.

The New Year

26

Come, let us anew
Our journey pursue,
Roll round with the year,
And never stand still, till the Master appear;
His adorable will
Let us gladly fulfil,
And our talents improve
By the patience of hope, and the labour of love.

Our life is a dream,
Our time, as a stream,
Glides swiftly away,
And the fugitive moment refuses to stay;
The arrow is flown,
The moment is gone,
The millennial year
Rushes on to our view, and eternity's here.

O that each in the day
Of His coming might say,
'I have fought my way through,
I have finished the work Thou didst give me to do!'
O that each from his Lord
May receive the glad word,
'Well and faithfully done,
Enter into My joy, and sit down on My throne!'

The Transfiguration

27

There appeared unto them Elias with Moses . . . Mark 9.4

Who Moses and the prophets hear,
　　And Christ the Sum of all receive,
Transfigured shall with Christ appear,
　　With Him in light and glory live,
Obtain a never-fading crown,
　　Enraptured on their Saviour gaze,
For ever by His side sit down,
　　And talk with Jesus face to face.

The Entry into Jerusalem

28

But they cried, saying, Crucify him. Luke 23.21

To David's Son and sovereign Lord
　　Hosanna *was* the people's cry,
Their King they yesterday adored,
　　Today they sentence Him to die:
So many blessings He bestowed,
　　So many wonders wrought in vain!
Such the benignity of God,
　　And such th' ingratitude of man!

29

In that sad memorable night,
    When Jesus was for us betrayed,
He left His death-recording rite,
    He took, and blessed, and brake the bread,
And gave His own their last bequest,
And thus His love's intent exprest:

Take, eat, this is My body, given
    To purchase life and peace for you,
Pardon and holiness and heaven;
    Do this My dying love to show,
Accept your precious legacy,
And thus, My friends, remember Me.

He took into His hands the cup,
    To crown the sacramental feast,
And full of kind concern looked up,
    And gave what He to them had blest;
And drink ye all of this, He said,
In solemn memory of the Dead.

This is my blood which seals the new
    Eternal covenant of My grace,
My blood so freely shed for you,
    For you and all the sinful race;
My blood that speaks your sins forgiven,
And justifies your claim to heaven.

The grace which I to all bequeath
  In this divine memorial take,
And, mindful of your Saviour's death,
  Do this, My followers, for My sake,
Whose dying love hath left behind
Eternal life for all mankind.

Passiontide

30

He loved, and gave Himself for me;
  On this, on this alone I build
My hope of life and liberty,
  And all the promises fulfilled.
His blood that purges every stain,
  Shall make me throughly clean and free;
And I shall love my Lord again,
  Who loved and gave Himself for me.

What may I not expect from Him,
  Who left for me His throne above?
He will from sin and death redeem
  The object of His dying love.
He will restore me from my fall,
  My pledge of heaven His passion is;
The bleeding cross hath promised all,
  And sworn my everlasting bliss.

My God, my God, why hast thou forsaken me?　Matthew 27.46

Who comprehends the reason why,
　　Must God's whole mystery explain,
Must know how all in Adam die,
　　That all may live in Christ again;
Must God's eternal purpose see,
　　(A secret to His host above,)
And sound the depths of Deity,
　　The wisdom, righteousness, and love.

Hast Thou forgot, Thou Man of woe,
　　The end of all Thy sorrows here,
For whom Thou didst Thy heaven forego,
　　For whom in mortal flesh appear?
Didst Thou not thirst to drink the cup,
　　T' accomplish Thy great sacrifice,
And yield Thy spotless spirit up,
　　And draw us after to the skies?

'Tis not for sin which Thou hast done,
　　Thine angry Father hides His face,
But on Thine innocence is shown
　　The vengeance due to Adam's race;
Thou all our sin and curse hast took,
　　That we may blessed and holy be;
Thou by Thy Father art forsook,
　　That God may ne'er abandon me.

O Love divine, what hast Thou done!
   Th' immortal God hath died for me!
The Father's co-eternal Son
   Bore all my sins upon the tree;
Th' immortal God for me hath died!
My Lord, my Love is crucified!

Behold Him, all ye that pass by,
   The bleeding Prince of Life and Peace!
Come, see, ye worms, your Maker die,
   And say, was ever grief like His?
Come, feel with me His blood applied:
My Lord, my Love is crucified!

Is crucified for me and you,
   To bring us rebels near to God;
Believe, believe the record true:
   We all are bought with Jesu's blood;
Pardon for all flows from His side;
My Lord, my Love is crucified!

Then let us sit beneath His cross,
   And gladly catch the healing stream,
All things for Him account but loss,
   And give up all our hearts to Him;
Of nothing speak or think beside,
'My Lord, my Love is crucified!'

33

'Christ the Lord is risen today,'
Sons of men and angels say!
Raise your joys and triumphs high;
Sing, ye heavens; and, earth, reply.

Love's redeeming work is done,
Fought the fight, the battle won:
Lo! our Sun's eclipse is o'er;
Lo! He sets in blood no more.

Vain the stone, the watch, the seal;
Christ has burst the gates of hell!
Death in vain forbids His rise:
Christ has opened paradise!

Lives again our glorious King:
Where, O death, is now thy sting?
Dying once, He all doth save:
Where thy victory, O grave?

Soar we now, where Christ has led?
Following our exalted Head,
Made like Him, like Him we rise,
Ours the cross, the grave, the skies!

What though once we perished all,
Partners in our parent's fall?
Second life we all receive,
In our heavenly Adam live.

Risen with Him, we upward move;
Still we seek the things above;
Still pursue, and kiss the Son
Seated on His Father's throne:

Scarce on earth a thought bestow,
Dead to all we leave below;
Heaven our aim, and loved abode,
Hid our life with Christ in God!

Hid; till Christ, our Life, appear,
Glorious in His members here:
Joined to Him, we then shall shine
All immortal, all divine!

Hail, the Lord of earth and heaven!
Praise to Thee by both be given:
Thee we greet triumphant now;
Hail, the Resurrection Thou!

King of Glory, Soul of bliss,
Everlasting life is this,
Thee to know, Thy power to prove,
Thus to sing, and thus to love!

34

He is not here: for he is risen, as he said.   Matthew 28.6

Who seek the Crucified,
    Dismiss your needless fear:
He once for sinners died,
    But lives no longer here:
This is the third triumphant day:
Come see the place where Jesus lay.

Among the dead in vain
　　Ye seek your heavenly Lord:
He lives, He lives again
　　According to His word!
Receive the power His life imparts,
And find Him risen in your hearts.

35

God hath both raised up the Lord, and will also raise up us by his own power.
1 Corinthians 6.14

Destroy this temple, and in three days I will raise it up. John 2.19

Christ . . . being put to death in the flesh, but quickened by the Spirit.
1 Peter 3.18

The breathless body of our Lord
　　Which once for sinners bled,
The blessed Trinity concurred
　　To raise it from the dead:
The Father did His Son restore
　　Uplifting from the grave,
And by His own effectual power
　　Life to Himself He gave.

The Spirit quickening Him, again
　　His soul and body joined;
And lo, in that immortal Man
　　The Triune God we find:
Each of the three is God alone,
　　The One almighty Lord,
One from eternity, and One
　　World without end adored.

Hail the day that sees Him rise,
Ravished from our wishful eyes!
Christ, awhile to mortals given,
Re-ascends His native heaven!

There the pompous triumph waits:
'Lift your heads, eternal gates,
Wide unfold the radiant scene,
Take the King of Glory in!'

Circled round with angel powers,
Their triumphant Lord, and ours,
Conqueror over death and sin,
Take the King of Glory in!

Him though highest heaven receives,
Still He loves the earth He leaves;
Though returning to His throne,
Still He calls mankind His own.

See! He lifts His hands above!
See! He shows the prints of love!
Hark! His gracious lips bestow
Blessings on His church below!

Still for us His death He pleads;
Prevalent, He intercedes;
Near Himself prepares our place,
Harbinger of human race.

Master, (will we ever say,)
Taken from our head today;
See Thy faithful servants, see!
Ever gazing up to Thee.

Grant, though parted from our sight,
High above yon azure height,
Grant our hearts may thither rise,
Following Thee beyond the skies.

Ever upward let us move,
Wafted on the wings of love;
Looking when our Lord shall come,
Longing, gasping after home.

There we shall with Thee remain,
Partners of Thy endless reign;
There Thy face unclouded see,
Find our heaven of heavens in Thee!

37

Christ is not entered into the holy places made with hands, which are the figures of the true; but into heaven itself, now to appear in the presence of God for us.
Hebrews 9.24

Entered the holy place above,
    Covered with meritorious scars,
The tokens of His dying love
    Our great High Priest in glory bears,
He pleads His passion on the tree,
He shows Himself to God for me.

Before the throne my Saviour stands,
    My Friend and Advocate appears;
My name is graven on His hands,
    And Him the Father always hears;
While low at Jesu's cross I bow,
He hears the blood of sprinkling now!

This instant now I may receive
    The answer of His powerful prayer:
This instant now by Him I live,
    His prevalence with God declare:
And soon my spirit in His hands
Shall stand, where my Forerunner stands!

Pentecost

38

Spirit of faith, on Thee we call,
    The merits of our Lord apply,
Convince, and then convert us all,
    Condemn, and freely justify;
Set forth the all-atoning Lamb,
And spread the powers of Jesu's name.

Jesus the merciful and just
    To every heart of man reveal,
In Him enable us to trust,
    Forgiveness through His blood to feel;
Let all in Him redemption find;
Sprinkle the blood on all mankind.

Is He not to His Father gone,
    That we His righteousness might share!
And art Thou not on earth sent down,
    The fruit of His prevailing prayer,
The witness of His grace, and seal,
The heavenly gift unspeakable!

O might we each receive the grace
    By Thee to call the Saviour *mine!*
Come, Holy Ghost, to all our race,
    Bring in the righteousness divine,
Inspire the sense of sin forgiven,
And give our earth a taste of heaven.

39

Blessed be God, even . . . the God of all comfort.   2 Corinthians 1.3

God of all consolation,
    The Holy Ghost Thou art,
Thy secret inspiration
    Hath told it to my heart:
The blessing I inherit,
    Through Jesus' prayer bestowed,
The Comforter, the Spirit,
    The true eternal God.

With God the Son and Saviour,
    With God the Father one,
The tokens of His favour
    Thou mak'st to sinners known,
An antepast of heaven
    Thou dost in me reveal,
Attest my sins forgiven,
    And my salvation seal.

Th' indubitable Witness
    Of Thy own deity,
Thou giv'st my soul its fitness
    Thy glorious face to see:
Thy comforts, gifts, and graces
    My largest thoughts transcend,
And challenge all my praises,
    When faith in sight shall end.

Trinity

40

Baptizing them in the name of the Father, and of the Son, and of the Holy Ghost.
Matthew 28.19

Baptized into one only name,
    The Father, Son, and Holy Ghost,
One nature we in three proclaim,
    One God for our salvation trust:
One God eternally abides,
    One undivided Trinity,
And the whole Deity resides
    In each of the mysterious three.

Each person properly divine,
    Co-equal in majestic power,
With all His heavenly host we join
    The great Jehovah to adore:
And worshipping the Triune God
    In confidence of humble love,
We soon shall reach His bright abode,
    And see His open face above.

Praise be to the Father given!
    Christ He gave
    Us to save,
Now the heirs of heaven.

Pay we equal adoration
    To the Son:
    He alone
Wrought out our salvation.

Glory to the eternal Spirit!
    Us He seals,
    Christ reveals,
And applies His merit.

Worship, honour, thanks, and blessing,
    One in Three,
    Give we Thee,
Never, never ceasing!

42

I heard the voice of the Lord, saying, Whom shall I send, and who will go for us?
Isaiah 6.8

Who Jehovah's mind hath known?
    Who His counsellor can be?
God requires advice of none,
    One inexplicable Three,
He Himself His council makes,
    All the glorious persons join,
Each the Deity partakes,
    Each is properly divine.

God is in you of a truth. 1 Corinthians 14.25

Christ is in you . . . 2 Corinthians 13.5

The Spirit . . . dwelleth with you, and shall be in you. John 14.17

God of a truth in us resides,
    Christ is in us both felt and known,
In us the Holy Ghost abides:
    Not three indwelling Gods, but one,
One true essential Deity
For ever one in persons three.

He that sent me is true. John 7.28

These things saith he that is . . . true, he that hath the key of David.
Revelation 3.7

The Spirit is truth. 1 John 5.6

Who sent the Son is true;
    True is the Son that came;
True is the Spirit too,
    Conferred in Jesus' name:
The Father, Son, and Holy Ghost
    Essential truth we own,
And prostrate with His heavenly host
    Adore the Three in One.

To Father, Son, and Holy Ghost,
Who sweetly all agree
To save a world of sinners lost,
Eternal glory be.

The Meeting of Friends

46

And are we yet alive,
And see each other's face?
Glory, and thanks to Jesus give
For His almighty grace:
Preserved by power divine
To full salvation here,
Again in Jesu's praise we join,
And in His sight appear.

What troubles have we seen,
What mighty conflicts past,
Fightings without, and fears within,
Since we assembled last!
Yet out of all the Lord
Hath brought us by His love,
And still He doth His help afford,
And hide our life above.

Then let us make our boast
Of His redeeming power,
Which saves us to the uttermost,
Till we can sin no more:
Let us take up the cross,
Till we the crown obtain,
And gladly reckon all things loss,
So we may Jesus gain.

Jesus to Thee we bow
And for Thy coming wait:
Give us for good some token now
In our imperfect state;
Apply the hallowing word,
Tell each who looks for Thee,
Thou shalt be perfect as thy Lord,
Thou shalt be all like Me!

3   Seven Psalms

Psalm 23 · Psalm 40 · Psalm 45 · Psalm 51
Psalm 70 · Psalm 117 (1739) · Psalm 117 (1743)

The Book of Psalms has always had an attraction for the Christian hymn writer. Metrical psalters existed long before anything we should recognize as a hymn book. John Julian in his *Dictionary of Hymnology* mentions one dating back to the eighth century; and lists Queen Elizabeth I as among those who tried their hands at turning the Psalms into English verse. He gives thirteen columns to the history of metrical psalmody, adding; 'With but few exceptions the succeeding pages are a comparison of mediocrities.'

Isaac Watts, whose *Hymns and Spiritual Songs* predates Charles Wesley's hymn writing by thirty years, gave much attention to how best the Book of Psalms (our Lord's own hymn book, and that of the early Church) could be adapted for fully Christian (i.e. New Testament) worship. He was concerned that 'by keeping too close to *David* in the House of God, the vail of *Moses* is thrown over our hearts'. In his first edition he included what he called 'A Short Essay Towards the Improvement of Psalmody: Or, an Enquiry how the Psalms of *David* ought to be translated into Christian Song, and how lawful and necessary it is to compose other hymns according to the clearer Revelations of the Gospel, for the Use of the Christian Church'. He went a good deal further in this process of 'translation' than most of his successors, or than accords with our mind today. 'Now if these be converted into Christian Songs in our nation,' he wrote, 'I think the names of *Ammon* and *Moab* may be properly chang'd into the names of the Chief Enemies of the Gospel so far as may be without public offence. *Judah* and *Israel* may be called *England* and *Scotland*, and the land of *Canaan* may be translated into *Great Britain*; the cloudy and typical Expressions of the Legal Dispensation shall be turned into Evangelical Language, according to the Explication of the New Testament . . .' The tempting invitation to identify the 'Chief Enemies of the Gospel' in the contemporary scene, and introduce their names into public worship, is enough to take one's breath away!

When we turn from Watts to Wesley, the scene changes. Wesley, I think, would make no claim that his hymns were *translations* of the Psalms, nor even in most cases *versions* of them. They are Christian hymns, based on the Psalms in the same way as he based some of his hymns on other writings, both from the Bible and from its commentators. So 'The Lord is my shepherd', which is the Authorized Version translation of Psalm 23, becomes simply 'Jesus the good Shepherd is' (*47*).

Of the seven Psalms that follow (taken from six originals, since *52* and *53* are based, for comparison, on the same short psalm) *50* is the best known in our modern hymnals, generally abbreviated. But *49*, 'My heart is full of Christ' is perhaps the most characteristic; in length, in metre (his favourite form, representing a tenth of his entire output, Frank Baker tells us) and in use of language. The latest Methodist hymn book *Hymns and Psalms* (1983) lists this as one of those hymns where the authorship is in dispute as between John and Charles; but I have felt it right (even against Dr Bett) to give to Charles the benefit of any doubt.

In the end, what matters in a hymn is not who wrote it, but what it says. Follow, then, in that long hymn the glorious progression from '*My* heart is full of Christ . . . *my* songs . . . *my* tongue . . . *my* King' in verse one, to the closing lines:

> . . . That all the world may learn Thy name:
> And all shall soon Thy grace adore,
> When time and sin shall be no more.

47

PSALM 23

Jesus the good Shepherd is;
   Jesus died the sheep to save;
He is mine, and I am His;
   All I want in Him I have –
Life, and health, and rest, and food,
All the plenitude of God.

Jesus loves and guards His own;
   Me in verdant pastures feeds;
Makes me quietly lie down,
   By the streams of comfort leads:
Following Him where'er He goes,
Silent joy my heart o'erflows.

He in sickness makes me whole,
   Guides into the paths of peace;
He revives my fainting soul,
   'Stablishes in righteousness;
Who for me vouchsafed to die,
Loves me still – I know not why!

Unappalled by guilty fear,
   Through the mortal vale I go;
My eternal Life is near;
   Thee my Life in death I know;
Bless Thy chastening, cheering rod,
Die into the arms of God!

Till that welcome hour I see,
    Thou before my foes dost feed;
Bidd'st me sit and feast with Thee,
    Pour'st Thy oil upon my head;
Giv'st me all I ask, and more,
Mak'st my cup of joy run o'er.

Love divine shall still embrace,
    Love shall keep me to the end;
Surely all my happy days
    I shall in Thy temple spend,
Till I to Thy house remove,
Thy eternal house above!

48

PSALM 40

PART I

Patient I waited for the Lord,
    Who heard and answered to my cry;
Out of the pit of sin, abhorred,
    He brought, and set me up on high:
Out of the mire and clay He took,
And fixed my feet upon a rock.

The Lord hath made my goings strong,
    And 'stablished me with gospel grace;
Put in my mouth the joyful song,
    The new, unceasing song of praise:
Many the deed divine shall see,
And fear, and trust in God, like me.

Blessed is the man that dares confide
    In my redeeming God alone:
O Lord, Thy works are multiplied,
    The wondrous works which Thou hast done!
Thy thoughts of grace to us surmount
The power of numbers to recount!

I cannot all Thy love declare;
    No, nor the smallest part express;
Worthless my noblest offerings are,
    Unfit the holy God to please;
But Thou dost unto me impart
A hearing ear, and loving heart.

No shadowy form dost Thou require,
    No legal sacrifice approve;
Thou seek'st the contrite heart's desire,
    The offering of obedient love;
And lo! I come to do Thy will,
And all Thy law in love fulfil!

Thy welcome will concerning me,
    I in the sacred volume read;
'Tis there my rule of life I see,
    And in Thy ways delight to tread;
While, by Thy love's divinest art,
Thy law is written on my heart.

Thine everlasting righteousness,
    Thou know'st I to Thy church have showed;
Nor hid within my heart the grace
    And goodness of my pardoning God:
Nor shunned in open thanks t' approve
The truth of Thy redeeming love.

The great salvation Thou hast wrought
    I have with joy to all declared:
Ah, gracious Lord! forsake me not,
    But let Thy tender mercies guard;
Thy faithful love my soul defend,
And save and keep me to the end!

PART II

For, O, my soul is sore beset
    By countless foes; encompassed round
By countless ills; beneath their weight
    I sink oppressed, o'erwhelmed, and bound;
The load immense I faint to bear,
And fails my heart through sad despair!

Help me! Thou God of love and might!
    Me to redeem make haste away:
Put all my cruel sins to flight,
    Slay all who seek my soul to slay;
Cover with shame my hater's face,
And all the alien armies chase.

Defeat the men, with Satan joined
    T' ensure my shame and misery;
Here only let the mockers find
    The dire reproach they cast on me;
Exploded, desolate, forlorn,
And wretched till to Thee they turn.

But let the men that seek Thy name
    Rejoice in Thee, their Lord and God;
The wonders of Thy love proclaim,
    And publish all Thy works abroad;
Saved by Thy dear redeeming grace,
And always happy in Thy praise.

I, too, the poorest sinner I,
    With them shall Thy compassion prove:
On Thee, my Saviour, I rely,
    And wait Thy succours from above:
Come, O my God, no more delay,
O come, and bring the perfect day!

49

PSALM 45

PART I

My heart is full of Christ, and longs
    Its glorious matter to declare!
Of Him I make my loftiest songs,
    I cannot from His praise forbear;
My ready tongue makes haste to sing
The beauties of my heavenly King.

Fairer than all the earth-born race,
    Perfect in comeliness Thou art;
Replenished are Thy lips with grace,
    And full of love Thy tender heart;
God ever blessed, we bow the knee,
And own all fulness dwells in Thee.

Gird on Thy thigh the Spirit's sword,
    And take to Thee Thy power divine,
Stir up Thy strength, almighty Lord!
    All power and majesty are Thine:
Assert Thy worship and renown,
O all-redeeming God, come down!

Come, and maintain Thy righteous cause,
    And let Thy glorious toil succeed;
Dispread the victory of Thy cross,
    Ride on, and prosper in Thy deed;
Through earth triumphantly ride on,
And reign in all our hearts alone.

Still let the word of truth prevail,
    The gospel of Thy general grace,
Of mercy mild that ne'er shall fail,
    Of everlasting righteousness,
Into the faithful soul brought in,
To root out all the seeds of sin.

Terrible things Thine own right hand
    Shall teach Thy greatness to perform:
Who in the vengeful day can stand
    Unshaken by Thine anger's storm,
While, riding on the whirlwind's wings,
They meet the thundering King of kings?

Sharp are the arrows of Thy love,
    And pierce the most obdurate heart:
Their point Thine enemies shall prove,
    And, strangely filled with pleasing smart,
Fall down before the cross subdued,
And feel Thine arrows dipped in blood.

O God of love, Thy sway we own,
    Thy dying love doth all control;
Justice and grace support Thy throne,
    Set up in every faithful soul;
Steadfast it stands in them, and sure,
When pure, as Thou their God art pure.

Lover Thou art of purity,
  And hatest every spot of sin;
Nothing profane can dwell with Thee,
  Nothing unholy or unclean:
And therefore doth Thy Father own
His glorious likeness in His Son.

Therefore He hath His Spirit shed,
  Spirit of joy, and power, and grace,
Immeasurably on Thy head;
  First-born of all the chosen race,
From Thee the sacred unction springs
That makes Thy fellows priests and kings.

PART II

Sweet is the odour of Thy name,
  Through all the means a fragrance comes;
Thy garments hide the sinner's shame,
  Thy garments shed divine perfumes,
That through the ivory palace flow –
The church, in which Thou reign'st below.

Thy heavenly charms the virgins move,
  And bow them to Thy pleasing sway;
They triumph in Thy princely love,
  Thy will with all their hearts obey;
Revere Thine honourable word,
The glorious handmaids of the Lord.

High above all, at Thy right hand,
  Adorned with each diviner grace,
Thy favourite queen exults to stand,
  Thy church her heavenly charms displays,
Clothed with the sun, for glory meet,
She sees the moon beneath her feet.

Daughter of heaven, though born on earth,
    Incline thy willing heart and ear;
Forget thy first ignoble birth,
    Thy people, and thy kinsfolk here;
So shall the King delight to see
His beauties copied out on thee.

He only is thy God and Lord;
    Worship divine to Him be given,
By all the host of heaven adored,
    By every creature under heaven;
And all the Gentile world shall know,
And freely to His service flow.

The rich shall lay their riches down,
    And poor become, for Jesu's sake;
Kings at His feet shall cast their crown,
    And humble suit for mercy make,
(Mercy alike on all bestowed,)
And languish to be great in God.

Are not His servants kings? and rule
    They not o'er hell, and earth, and sin?
His daughter is divinely full
    Of Christ, and 'glorious all within;'
    All glorious inwardly she reigns,
And not one spot of sin remains.

Clothed with humility and love,
    With every dazzling virtue bright,
With faith which God vouchsafes t' approve,
    Precious in her great Father's sight,
The royal maid with joy shall come,
Triumphant, to her heavenly home.

Brought by His sweet attracting grace,
　　She first shall in His sight appear
In holiness before His face,
　　Made perfect with her fellows here:
Spotless and pure, a virgin train,
They all shall in His palace reign.

In lieu of seers and patriarchs old,
　　Of whom she once did make her boast,
The virgin-mother shall behold
　　Her numerous sons a princely host,
Installed o'er all the earth abroad,
Anointed kings and priests to God.

Thee, Jesus, King of kings, and Lord
　　Of lords, I glory to proclaim;
From age to age Thy praise record,
　　That all the world may learn Thy name:
And all shall soon Thy grace adore,
When time and sin shall be no more.

50

PSALM 51

O for an heart to praise my God,
　　An heart from sin set free!
An heart that always feels Thy blood,
　　So freely spilt for me!

An heart resigned, submissive, meek,
　　My dear Redeemer's throne,
Where only Christ is heard to speak,
　　Where Jesus reigns alone.

An humble, lowly, contrite heart,
  Believing, true, and clean,
Which neither life nor death can part
  From Him that dwells within.

An heart in every thought renewed,
  And full of love divine,
Perfect, and right, and pure, and good,
  A copy, Lord, of Thine.

Thy tender heart is still the same,
  And melts at human woe:
Jesu, for Thee distrest I am,
  I want Thy love to know.

My heart, Thou know'st, can never rest,
  Till Thou create my peace;
Till, of my Eden repossest,
  From self and sin I cease.

Fruit of Thy gracious lips, on me
  Bestow that peace unknown,
The hidden manna, and the tree
  Of life, and the white stone.

Thy nature, dearest Lord, impart;
  Come quickly from above;
Write Thy new name upon my heart,
  Thy new, best name of Love.

51

PSALM 70

Jesu, mighty to deliver,
  Help afford, Hasten, Lord,
    Or I die for ever.

Those that have my soul surrounded,
  Let them flee, Chased by Thee,
    Baffled, and confounded.

But let all who seek Thy favour
  Hear Thy voice, And rejoice
    In their present Saviour.

Those whose earnest expectation
  Waits for Thee, Let them see
    All Thy great salvation.

Let their lips show forth Thy glory,
  Full of praise, For Thy grace
    Let their hearts adore Thee.

O might I with these confess Thee!
  Needy I, Fain would try
    With Thy saints to bless Thee!

Hasten, Lord, my soul deliver;
  Thou art mine, Seal me Thine,
    Seal me Thine for ever.

52

PSALM 117 (1739)

Ye nations, who the globe divide,
Ye numerous nations scattered wide,
   To God your grateful voices raise:
To all His boundless mercy shown,
His truth to endless ages known
   Require our endless love and praise.

To Him who reigns enthroned on high,
To His dear Son who deigned to die
   Our guilt and errors to remove;
To that blest Spirit who grace imparts,
Who rules in all believing hearts,
   Be ceaseless glory, praise, and love!

53

PSALM 117 (1743)

Praise the Lord, ye ransomed nations,
   God of universal grace;
Him, with joyful acclamations,
   All ye sons of Adam, praise!

Jesus, mighty to deliver,
   Bids you all His mercy prove;
Jesu's truth endures for ever,
   Praise Him for His faithful love.

4 Church and Ministry

The Church of God · Ministers of Christ · God's invitation
The Lord's Supper

In the Minutes of the Methodist Conference for 1788 there
appears this entry:

Who have died this year? . . .
5. Mr Charles Wesley, who, after spending four score years
with much sorrow and pain, quietly retired into Abraham's
bosom. He had no disease; but, after a gradual decay of some
months,

The weary wheels of life stood still at last.

His least praise was his talent for poetry: although Dr Watts
did not scruple to say, that 'that single poem, *Wrestling Jacob*,
was worth all the verses he himself had written'.

At first sight it seems a remarkable, even a back-handed
tribute, to one so signally gifted. The explanation surely lies in
the day-to-day ministry which Charles pursued, in company
with his brother John, as a preacher of the gospel and one of the
leaders of the Society. Year after year, steadily, Charles's early
journal records his travels and labours; the opposition of mobs
on the one hand and of his fellow clergy on the other. Day after
day found him faithfully preaching, expounding, exhorting and
'tending the flock'. We can understand that in the eyes of his
contemporaries even the exercise of his remarkable gift was not
as praiseworthy as the faithful testimony of his life and work.

John Telford, one of his earlier biographers, gives what he
calls 'a sketch of his work' during a single year, 1743:

On Sunday morning, January 2nd, he rode to Bexley and
preached there; then returned to conduct service at the
Foundery. Next day he was at Brentford and Eton. On
Wednesday he reached Bristol, where he remained till the
following Tuesday morning, when he set out for London at

three o'clock. He reached the Foundery next day. In London he remained six weeks, visiting the prisoners in Newgate and supplying the Methodist pulpits; then he returned to Bath. In the middle of May he visited the north of England, where he laboured amid the hottest persecution. During his six weeks' journey he visited more than thirty places, including Wednesbury, Walsall, Birmingham, Nottingham, Sheffield, Birstal, Leeds, Newcastle, Sunderland, Shields, Epworth, and Oxford. After a busy fortnight in London, he went through Bristol to Exeter and Cornwall, then the scene of fierce and constant riots. A month later he returned to London for two months of scarcely less exhausting work. He then journeyed northwards again to meet his brother at Nottingham. On October 29th he was in Bristol, where he had only spent one day during the last six months. His friends in that city kept him two days. Then he visited Wales. The last month of the year was spent in London.

It is against this background of controversy for the truth, and his own deep love of the Church of England from which he had no thought of separating (and never did) that 54 and 55 should be read. Charles's view of the Christian ministry, shaped by the New Testament, invited the inevitable comparison between his own and his brother's labours and the prevailing standards among many (if not most) clergy of his day. I have included the *jeu d'esprit*, *64*, to illuminate another side to his character; the title given in *The Poetical Works* is 'Written (in short hand) during a journey from London to Norwich, July, 1754.'

The final verses in this section, on 'The Lord's Supper', are representatives of a theme to which Charles Wesley constantly returned. For this precious sacrament he had a mystical and profound reverence, publishing in 1745 his *Hymns on the Lord's Supper* from which these (together with *29*) are taken.

54

CATHOLICK LOVE

Weary of all this wordy strife,
   These notions, forms, and modes, and names,
To Thee, the Way, the Truth, the Life,
   Whose love my simple heart inflames,
Divinely taught, at last I fly,
With Thee, and Thine to live, and die.

Forth from the midst of Babel brought,
   Parties and sects I cast behind;
Enlarged my heart, and free my thought,
   Where'er the latent truth I find,
The latent truth with joy to own,
And bow to Jesu's name alone.

Redeemed by Thine almighty grace,
   I taste my glorious liberty,
With open arms the world embrace,
   But cleave to those who cleave to Thee;
But only in Thy saints delight,
Who walk with God in purest white.

One with the little flock I rest,
   The members sound who hold the Head;
The chosen few, with pardon blest,
   And by th' anointing Spirit led
Into the mind that was in Thee,
Into the depths of Deity.

My brethren, friends, and kinsmen these,
    Who do my heavenly Father's will;
Who aim at perfect holiness,
    And all Thy counsels to fulfil,
Athirst to be whate'er Thou art,
And love their God with all their heart.

For these, howe'er in flesh disjoined,
    Where'er dispersed o'er earth abroad,
Unfeigned unbounded love I find,
    And constant as the life of God;
Fountain of life, from thence it sprung,
As pure, as even, and as strong.

Joined to the hidden church unknown
    In this sure bond of perfectness,
Obscurely safe, I dwell alone,
    And glory in th' uniting grace,
To me, to each believer given,
To all Thy saints in earth and heaven.

55

A PRAYER FOR THE CHURCH OF ENGLAND

Head of Thy church, attend
    Our long-continued prayer,
And our Jerusalem defend,
    And in Thy bosom bear
The sheep of England's fold,
    Marked with their Shepherd's sign,
Bought with a price, redeemed of old,
    And washed in blood divine.

Called out of Babylon
At Thy command they came;
Our ancestors their lives laid down,
And triumphed in the flame:
The Church's seed arose
Out of the martyrs' blood,
And saw their anti-Christian foes
Before Thy cross subdued.

Again Thy Spirit of grace
Doth with our Israel strive,
And even in our degenerate days
His ancient work revive.
Ten thousand witnesses
Stand forth on every side,
And, bold in life and death, confess
Jehovah crucified.

O that the faithful seed
May never, never fail,
Victorious through their conquering Head
O'er all the powers of hell!
Still with Thy people stay,
By England's Church adored,
Till every island flee away
Before our glorious Lord.

56

Other foundation can no man lay . . .   1 Corinthians 3.11

Christ is the one Foundation laid,
   In the deep counsels of the Lord,
In promises to sinners made,
   In the inspired, prophetic word,
In welcome news of peace divine,
In all His people's hearts and mine.

Him Prophet, Priest, and King we own,
   Essential God, and real man;
The church is built on Christ alone,
   Its doctrines, discipline, and plan;
Its duties and its blessings rise
On Him, the Lord of earth and skies.

Rock of eternity, He stood
   Immovable in steadfast grace,
Beneath the utmost wrath of God,
   Beneath the sin of Adam's race;
And still my faith's support remains,
And still He all my load sustains.

Sole basis of our faith and hope,
   We on His life and death rely,
His death from hell shall lift us up,
   His life shall bear us to the sky,
Entitled, fitted for the place,
By Jesus' blood and righteousness.

[72]

57

Lord of the gospel harvest, send
  More labourers forth into Thy field,
More pastors teach Thy flock to tend,
  More workmen raise Thy house to build;
His work, and place, to each assign,
And clothe their word with power divine.

But chiefly to Thy mild command
  The masters of our Israel bow:
Stars let them shine in Thy right hand
  (Eclipsed, alas! and wandering now!)
Who do not yet Thy kingdom see,
But ask, How can the mystery be?

Light of the world, Thy beams impart,
  To make Thy witnesses appear;
Thy Spirit shining in the heart
  Appoints the gospel minister:
Now, Lord, the gracious wonder show,
An Angel on Thy church bestow.

Moved by our long continued cry,
  Some apostolic father raise,
Our want of labourers to supply,
  T' admit the vessels of Thy grace,
To lay on hands, o'erruled by Thine,
And recognise the call divine.

The Holy Ghost hath made you overseers.   Acts 20.28

Who but the Holy Ghost can make
    The genuine gospel-minister,
The bishop, bold to undertake
    Of precious souls the awful care?
The Holy Ghost alone can move
    A sinner, sinners to convert,
Infuse the apostolic love,
    And bless him with a pastor's heart.

Not all the hands of all mankind
    Can constitute one overseer;
But spirited with Jesu's mind,
    The heavenly messengers appear,
They follow close with zeal divine
    The Bishop great, the Shepherd good,
And cheerfully their lives resign
    To save the purchase of His blood.

59

Jesus, Thy servants bless,
    Who sent by Thee proclaim
The peace, and joy, and righteousness,
    Experienced in Thy name;
    The kingdom of our God
    Which Thy great Spirit imparts,
The power of Thy victorious blood
    Which reigns in faithful hearts.

Our souls with faith supply,
With life and liberty;
And lo, we preach and testify
The things concerning Thee;
We live for this alone,
Thy grace to minister,
And all Thou hast for sinners done
In life and death declare.

60

Pray ye therefore the Lord of the harvest, that he will send forth labourers into his harvest. Matthew 9.38

So they, being sent forth by the Holy Ghost . . . Acts 13.4

Holy Ghost, regard our prayers,
Third of the glorious Three,
Send forth faithful labourers
To gather souls for Thee:
Sovereign, everlasting Lord,
The harvest is entirely Thine,
Thine the preachers of the word,
The messengers divine.

Move their hearts, and more stir up
Salvation to proclaim,
Bold on every mountain-top
To shout in Jesus' name,
Tidings of great joy to tell,
Of peace obtained, and sin forgiven;
Then, Thy word of grace to seal,
O God, come down from heaven.

61

Here am I; send me.   Isaiah 6.8

Ah, woe is me, immersed in sin,
A man of lips and life unclean!
How shall I with Thy message run,
Or preach the pardoning God unknown?
Unless my God vouchsafe to cheer
His guilty trembling messenger,
My fears disperse, my sins remove,
And purge me by the fire of love!

O wouldst Thou touch my lips once more,
The comfort of Thy grace restore,
Assure me, Lord, that mine Thou art,
And stamp forgiveness on my heart;
Then should I in *my* Jesu's name
Glad tidings of great joy proclaim,
Of grace, which every soul may find,
And glory bought for all mankind.

62

For the work whereunto I have called them . . .   Acts 13.2

Christ's ministers apart are set
For work, not idleness or state,
    For toils that never cease;
By Him in all their labours blessed
Till Jesus gives His servants rest
    And bids them die in peace.

The Lord appointed other seventy also. Luke 10.1

Two and two, not one and one,
    He sends His messengers,
Makes by them His coming known,
    By them His way prepares:
What shall part whom God hath joined,
    Or break th' indissoluble cord?
Two are one in heart and mind,
    When Jesus is the third.

64

    In the name of the Lord,
    And the strength of His word,
    A-fishing we go:
This our only delight and employment below.
    As fishing for men
    Our labour again
    With joy we repeat,
And again, till we catch the whole race in our net.

    With the blessing divine
    On our net and our line,
    We labour for souls;
And at Jesu's command we shall take them in shoals.
    On the right we shall cast,
    And catch them at last,
    If our toil He approve,
With the hook of His power, and the bait of His love.

O Saviour, be nigh
Thy word to apply,
Thy gospel to bless,
And crown our attempts with abundant success!
The profligate poor
With a pardon allure
Their Lord to embrace,
And captivate all with the offers of grace.

With favour look on,
While we let the net down,
Down into the deep,
And enclose such a number as sinks the old ship.
Nor shall our hearts shrink
Though the vessel should sink:
Nor will we repine,
To be lost in an ocean of mercy divine.

65

AFTER PREACHING

Glory, and praise, and love to Thee,
    For this effectual door,
Jesu! who publishest by me
    The gospel to the poor.

Glory to Thy great name alone,
    That life and power imparts:
Now, Lord, Thy genuine gospel own,
    And graft it on their hearts.

Now let them feel the tidings true,
  Grant to Thy word success;
Water it with Thy heavenly dew,
  And give the wished increase.

Savour of life, O, let it prove,
  And show their sins forgiven;
Work in them faith, which works by love,
  And surely leads to heaven.

66

AFTER PREACHING IN A CHURCH

Jesu, accept the grateful song,
  My Wisdom and my Might,
'Tis Thou hast loosed the stammering tongue,
  And taught my hands to fight.

Thou, Jesus, Thou my mouth hast been;
  The weapons of Thy war,
Mighty through Thee, I pull down sin,
  And all Thy truth declare.

Not without Thee, my Lord, I am
  Come up unto this place,
Thy Spirit bade me preach Thy name,
  And trumpet forth Thy praise.

Thy Spirit gave me utterance now,
  My soul with strength endued,
Hardened to adamant my brow,
  And armed my heart with God.

Thy powerful hand in all I see,
　　Thy wondrous workings own,
Glory, and strength, and praise to Thee
　　Ascribe, and Thee alone.

Gladly I own the promise true
　　To all whom Thou dost send,
'Behold I always am with you,
　　Your Saviour to the end!'

Amen, amen, my God and Lord,
　　If Thou art with me still,
I still shall speak the gospel word,
　　My ministry fulfil.

Thee I shall constantly proclaim,
　　Though earth and hell oppose,
Bold to confess Thy glorious name
　　Before a world of foes.

Jesus the name, high over all
　　In hell, or earth, or sky,
Angels and men before it fall,
　　And devils fear, and fly.

Jesus, the name to sinners dear,
　　The name to sinners given,
It scatters all their guilty fear,
　　And turns their hell to heaven.

Balm into wounded spirits it pours,
　　And heals the sin-sick mind;
It hearing to the deaf restores,
　　And eyesight to the blind.

Jesus the prisoner's fetters breaks,
 And bruises Satan's head,
Power into strengthless souls it speaks,
 And life into the dead.

O that the world might taste, and see
 The riches of His grace!
The arms of love which compass me,
 Would all mankind embrace.

O that my Jesu's heavenly charms
 Might every bosom move!
Fly sinners, fly into those arms
 Of everlasting love.

The Lover of your souls is near,
 Him I to you commend,
Joyful the Bridegroom's voice to hear,
 Who calls a worm His friend.

He hath the bride, and He alone,
 Almighty to redeem,
I only make His mercies known,
 I send you all to Him.

Sinners, behold the Lamb of God,
 On Him your spirits stay;
He bears the universal load,
 He takes your sins away.

His only righteousness I show,
 His saving grace proclaim;
'Tis all my business here below
 To cry, Behold the Lamb!

For this a suffering life I live,
    And reckon all things loss;
For Him my strength, my all I give,
    And glory in His cross.

I spend myself, that you may know
    The Lord our righteousness,
That Christ in you may live, and grow,
    I joyfully decrease.

Gladly I hasten to decay,
    My life I freely spend,
And languish for the welcome day,
    When all my toil shall end.

Happy, if with my latest breath
    I might but gasp His name,
Preach Him to all, and cry in death
    Behold, behold the Lamb!

67

THE PRAYER OF A DEPARTING MINISTER

Shepherd of souls, the great, the good,
Who on Thy servant's side hast stood,
    And blessed my ministry,
Ready my prospered course to end,
I to Thy guardian love commend
    The flock received from Thee.

Beneath Thy wings, their sure defence,
Protected by Omnipotence,
    Thy most distinguished care,
The lambs and sheep of England's fold
Now in the book of life enrolled
    Preserve for ever there.

Our church a thousandfold increase,
With every gospel-blessing bless,
    And o'er the earth disperse,
Till every heart Thy kingdom own,
Till Thou art feared, confessed, and known
    Throughout the universe.

In hope of that most joyful day,
To quit this tenement of clay
    Thy summons I receive,
For when I lay my body down
Thy work shall still be carried on,
    And God for ever live.

The Spirit's residue is Thine:
Fit instruments of Thy design,
    Dispensers of Thy grace,
(If some, like salt, their savour lose,)
Thou canst from other stones produce,
    And nobler vessels raise.

Come then, Thy servant to release,
And suffered to depart in peace,
    Without a lingering sigh,
In all the confidence of hope
I now ascend the mountain-top,
    And get me up and die.

A PRAYER FOR THE BISHOPS

Draw near, O Son of God, draw near,
  Us with Thy flaming eyes behold,
Still in Thy falling church appear,
  And let our candlestick be gold.

Still hold the stars in Thy right hand,
  And let them in Thy lustre glow,
The lights of a benighted land,
  The angels of Thy church below.

Make good their apostolic boast,
  Their high commission let them prove,
Be temples of the Holy Ghost,
  And filled with faith, and hope, and love.

The worthy successors of those
  Who first adorned the sacred line,
Bold let them stand before their foes,
  And dare assert their right divine.

Their hearts from things of earth remove;
  Sprinkle them, Lord, from sin and fear!
Fix their affections all above,
  And lay up all their treasure there.

Give them an ear to hear the word
  Thou speakest to Thy churches now;
And let all tongues confess their Lord,
  And let all knees to Jesus bow.

God's invitation

69

All ye that pass by,
To Jesus draw nigh:
To you is it nothing that Jesus should die?
Your ransom and peace,
Your surety He is,
Come, see if there ever was sorrow like His.

For what you have done
His blood must atone:
The Father hath punished for you His dear Son.
The Lord in the day
Of His anger did lay
Your sins on the Lamb; and He bore them away.

He answered for all,
O come at His call,
And low at His cross with astonishment fall.
But lift up your eyes
At Jesus's cries:
Impassive He suffers, immortal He dies.

He dies to atone
For sins not His own;
Your debt He hath paid, and your work He hath done.
Ye all may receive
The peace He did leave,
Who made intercession 'My Father forgive!'

For you, and for me
He prayed on the tree,
The prayer is accepted, the sinner is free.
The sinner am I,
Who on Jesus rely,
And come for the pardon God cannot deny.

My pardon I claim,
For a sinner I am,
A sinner believing in Jesus's name.
He purchased the grace,
Which now I embrace:
O Father, Thou know'st He hath died in my place.

His death is my plea,
My Advocate see,
And hear the blood speak that hath answered for me.
Acquitted I was,
When He bled on the cross,
And by losing His life He hath carried my cause.

70

Ho, every one that thirsteth, come ye to the waters . . .   Isaiah 55.1

Come all the lost race, Redeemed from your fall;
A fountain of grace Is opened for all:
Your God's invitation Discovers the stream;
The wells of salvation Are opened in Him.

Who seek to be blessed, But labour in vain,
And sigh for the rest Ye cannot attain,
Come all to the Saviour, Your life-giving Lord,
And find in His favour Your Eden restored.

Poor vagabonds here Who shadows pursue,
To Jesus draw near For happiness true.
Ye all may receive it, (Good news for the poor,)
And when ye believe it, Your pardon is sure.

Come, taste, and confess The goodness divine,
The sense of His grace Is better than wine:
'Tis sweeter than honey, The milk of the word;
'Tis bought without money, The love of your Lord.

No goodness have ye, No goodness ye need;
His mercy is free, Is mercy indeed!
Renounce your own merit, And buy without price
His grace and His Spirit, And crown in the skies.

Distracted by thought And care without end,
Your labour for nought, Ah! why will ye spend,
Your time of probation In trifles employ,
In vain expectation Of fugitive joy?

For pleasure, and praise, And riches ye pant;
Your wishes possess, Yet perish for want:
Destroyed by fruition, Your bliss ye bemoan,
And wail your condition, Contented with none.

Come just as ye are, For Jesus invites
Mere sinners to share Substantial delights:
Ye weary, and burdened, Who happy would be,
And wish to be pardoned, Come, listen to Me.

Be blessed for My sake, With permanent good
And freely partake Angelical food,
Be fed by believing With bread from above,
My nature receiving, And filled with My love.

The ear of your heart, Whoever incline,
To you I impart My fulness divine,
Your souls by My Spirit Made meet for the sky,
The life shall inherit, Which never shall die.

The Lord's Supper

71

Author of life divine,
　　Who hast a table spread,
Furnished with mystic wine
　　And everlasting bread,
Preserve the life Thyself hast given,
And feed and train us up for heaven.

Our needy souls sustain
　　With fresh supplies of love,
Till all Thy life we gain,
　　And all Thy fulness prove,
And, strengthened by Thy perfect grace,
Behold without a veil Thy face.

72

Victim divine, Thy grace we claim
　　While thus Thy precious death we show;
Once offered up, a spotless Lamb,
　　In Thy great temple here below,
Thou didst for all mankind atone,
And standest now before the throne.

Thou standest in the holiest place,
   As now for guilty sinners slain;
Thy blood of sprinkling speaks, and prays,
   All-prevalent for helpless man;
Thy blood is still our ransom found,
And spreads salvation all around.

The smoke of Thy atonement here
   Darkened the sun and rent the veil,
Made the new way to heaven appear,
   And showed the great Invisible;
Well pleased in Thee our God looked down,
And called His rebels to a crown.

He still respects Thy sacrifice,
   Its savour sweet doth always please;
The offering smokes through earth and skies,
   Diffusing life, and joy, and peace;
To these Thy lower courts it comes,
And fills them with divine perfumes.

We need not now go up to heaven,
   To bring the long-sought Saviour down;
Thou art to all already given,
   Thou dost e'en now Thy banquet crown:
To every faithful soul appear,
And show Thy real presence here!

73

Happy the man to whom 'tis given
To eat the bread of life in heaven:
This happiness in Christ we prove,
Who feed on His forgiving love.

74

Come, Holy Ghost, Thine influence shed,
  And realize the sign;
Thy life infuse into the bread,
  Thy power into the wine.

Effectual let the tokens prove,
  And made, by heavenly art,
Fit channels to convey Thy love
  To every faithful heart.

75

Jesu, on Thee we feed
  Along the desert way,
Thou art the living Bread
  Which doth our spirits stay,
And all who in this banquet join
Lean on the staff of life divine.

While to Thy upper courts
  We take our joyful flight,
Thy blessed cross supports
  Each feeble Israelite;
Like hoary dying Jacob we
Lean on our staff and worship Thee.

O may we still abide
  In Thee our pardoning God,
Thy Spirit be our guide,
  Thy body be our food,
Till Thou who hast the token given
Shalt bear us on Thyself to heaven.

5 The Life of Faith

Penitence · Grace and salvation · Trust in God
Abiding in Christ · Following Christ
Trial and temptation · The Christian warfare
Prayer and the Scriptures · Love, joy, peace
Praise and thanksgiving

In his Introduction to *The Penguin Book of English Christian Verse*
Peter Levi gives his opinion that 'the worst fault of any poetry,
particularly religious poetry, is a certain falsity, an archaism and
formality that pretend to a spirit they are not quite able to
summon up.' Of this Charles Wesley is entirely free. Dr Bett
described his style as 'a remarkable phenomenon . . . distinctly
and strikingly the most modern style of the period'; and many
have seen in him one of the heralds of the Romantic Revival.
Similarly, there is no formality or falsity in his hymnody,
because it is rooted in his own spiritual experience. Before he
sang about the life of faith, he lived it.

In the poems that follow, *79* echoes the continuing conflict
between the Wesleys with their gospel of free grace to all, and
the extreme Calvinism of their day. One can see how, by the use
of italics and capital letters (over seventy words italicised, and
the words 'Hellish Doctrine' in very bold black capitals)
Charles drummed home his point. Here is verse three as it first
appeared in *Hymns on God's Everlasting Love* in 1741:

> Thy *Undistinguishing* Regard
>   Was cast on *Adam's* fallen Race:
> *For All* Thou hast in CHRIST prepar'd
>   *Sufficient, Sovereign, Saving* Grace.

These seventeen verses stand unequalled, perhaps, as a
sustained and impassioned declaration of their theme.

Numbers *87* and *88*, to be found in most contemporary
hymnbooks, form an example of Charles Wesley's ability to

draw from the Old Testament a spiritual harvest for the Christian worshipper. Both these hymns are clearly written with Matthew Henry's *Commentary* open before him, or else in the very forefront of his mind. Compare *87* with Henry's note on Leviticus 8: 'We have every one of us *a charge to keep*, an eternal *God to glorify*, *an immortal soul* to provide for . . . *our generation to serve*; and it must be our daily *care* to keep this charge, for it is the charge of the Lord our *Master*, who will shortly call us to *account* about it . . . (italics mine).' Even more striking is a similar comparison between Henry and *88*, where the correspondence (often, but not always in identical words) can be seen in eleven of the sixteen lines. But then Charles Wesley's hymns have been described as 'a mosaic of biblical allusions'; and it should be no surprise to discover that in the same two short hymns the most recent editors have noted echoes of eighteen other books of the Bible.

In 'Jesu, Lover of my soul' and 'Soldiers of Christ, arise' (*92* and *94*) it is interesting to compare the hymns as Charles Wesley wrote them with the well-known versions in our current hymnbooks. The first of these did not find a place in his *Collection* while John Wesley was alive; it is said, because of the word 'Lover' as applied to the Lord Jesus Christ – even though this is derived from the Apocrypha. More striking still is the word 'panoply' in *94* which is a quotation not from the English ('the *whole armour* of God') of Ephesian 6.11 and 13, but from the Greek New Testament, where the word used is *panoplia*.

Part of the secret, surely, of the continued use of Charles Wesley's hymns in all branches of today's Church (including the Roman Catholic) lies in the fact that they still speak to our condition. No one can have progressed far in the life of faith without discovering a mirror to personal experience in the poems that follow.

76

If we confess our sins, he is faithful and just to forgive us our sins, and to cleanse us . . . 1 John 1.9

Father of Jesus Christ our Lord,
    Our sins we in His name confess;
Righteous and faithful to Thy word,
    From actual guilt our souls release;
And purge out all this filth within,
And make our inward nature clean.

If still, when justified by grace,
    Our general sinfulness we own,
Thou wilt on us Thy name impress,
    Reveal the nature of Thy Son;
And write it on our inward parts,
And spread Thine image through our hearts.

Wherefore Thy goodness we implore
    A deeper sense of sin to give,
That small in our own eyes, and poor,
    We may Thy richest grace receive;
May always in Thy Son abide,
May always feel His blood applied.

Soon as we every moment feel
    Ourselves vile nothings in Thy sight,
In Christ we every moment dwell,
    Blameless we walk with Him in white,
His perfect purity retain,
And never soil our robes again.

Stay, Thou insulted Spirit stay,
   Though I have done Thee such despite,
Nor cast the sinner quite away,
   Nor take Thine everlasting flight.

Though I have steeled my stubborn heart,
   And still shook off my guilty fears,
And vexed and urged Thee to depart
   For forty long rebellious years:

Though I have most unfaithful been,
   Of all whoe'er Thy grace received,
Ten thousand times Thy goodness seen,
   Ten thousand times Thy goodness grieved:

Yet O! the chief of sinners spare,
   In honour of my great High Priest,
Nor in Thy righteous anger swear
   T' exclude me from Thy people's rest.

This only woe I deprecate,
   This only plague, I pray, remove,
Nor leave me in my lost estate,
   Nor curse me with this want of love.

If yet Thou canst my sins forgive,
   From now, O Lord, relieve my woes,
Into Thy rest of love receive,
   And bless me with the calm repose.

From now my weary soul release,
   Upraise me by Thy gracious hand,
And guide into Thy perfect peace,
   And bring me to the promised land.

And Jesus was left alone, and the woman . . .   John 8.9

The gospel stands in Moses' place:
The foes of Jesus and His grace
 Are scattered by a word,
Th' accusers all are fled and gone,
Misery with mercy left alone,
 The sinner with her Lord.

If left alone with Thee I am,
Though covered o'er with guilt and shame,
 I nothing have to fear;
My Saviour in my Judge I meet,
And wait a sinner at Thy feet,
 Thy pardoning voice to hear.

Grace and salvation

79

Father, whose everlasting love
 Thy only Son for sinners gave,
Whose grace to all did freely move,
 And sent Him down a world to save:

Help us Thy mercy to extol,
 Immense, unfathomed, unconfined;
To praise the Lamb who died for all,
 The general Saviour of mankind.

Thy undistinguishing regard
  Was cast on Adam's fallen race;
For all Thou hast in Christ prepared
  Sufficient, sovereign, saving grace.

Jesus hath said, we all shall hope,
  Preventing grace for all is free:
'And I, if I be lifted up,
  I will draw all men unto Me.'

What soul those drawings never knew?
  With whom hath not Thy Spirit strove?
We all must own that God is true,
  We all may feel that God is love.

O all ye ends of earth, behold
  The bleeding, all-atoning Lamb!
Look unto Him for sinners sold,
  Look and be saved through Jesu's name.

Behold the Lamb of God, who takes
  The sins of all the world away!
His pity no exception makes;
  But all that will receive Him, may.

A world He suffered to redeem;
  For all He hath th' atonement made:
For those that will not come to Him
  The ransom of His life was paid.

Their Lord, unto His own He came;
  His own were who received Him not,
Denied and trampled on His name
  And blood, by which themselves were bought.

Who under foot their Saviour trod,
    Exposed afresh, and crucified,
Who trampled on the Son of God –
    For them, for them, their Saviour died.

For those who at the judgment day
    On Him they pierced shall look with pain;
The Lamb for every castaway,
    For every soul of man was slain.

Why then, Thou universal Love,
    Should any of Thy grace despair?
To all, to all, Thy bowels move,
    But straitened in our own we are.

'Tis we, the wretched abjects we,
    Our blasphemies on Thee translate;
We think that fury is in Thee,
    Horribly think, that God is hate.

'Thou hast compelled the lost to die,
    Hast reprobated from Thy face;
Hast others saved, but them passed by,
    Or mocked with only damning grace.'

How long, Thou jealous God! how long
    Shall impious worms Thy word disprove,
Thy justice stain, Thy mercy wrong,
    Deny Thy faithfulness and love?

Still shall the hellish doctrine stand,
    And Thee for its dire author claim?
No: let it sink at Thy command
    Down to the pit from whence it came.

Arise, O God, maintain Thy cause!
  The fulness of the Gentiles call:
Lift up the standard of Thy cross,
  And all shall own Thou diedst for all.

80

    The one religion see
      Which God vouchsafes t' approve,
  'Tis grounded on His unity,
        'Tis – Hear, believe, and love!

81

Thou God of glorious majesty,
To Thee against myself, to Thee
  A worm of earth I cry,
An half-awakened child of man,
An heir of endless bliss or pain,
  A sinner born to die.

Lo! on a narrow neck of land,
'Twixt two unbounded seas I stand
  Secure, insensible:
A point of life, a moment's space
Removes me to that heavenly place,
  Or shuts me up in hell.

O God, mine inmost soul convert,
And deeply on my thoughtful heart
  Eternal things impress,
Give me to feel their solemn weight,
And tremble on the brink of fate,
  And wake to righteousness.

Before me place in dread array
The pomp of that tremendous day,
    When Thou with clouds shalt come
To judge the nations at Thy bar:
And tell me, Lord, shall I be there
    To meet a *joyful* doom?

Be this my one great business here,
With serious industry, and fear,
    My future bliss t' insure,
Thine utmost counsel to fulfil,
And suffer all Thy righteous will,
    And to the end endure.

Then, Saviour, then my soul receive,
Transported from the vale, to live,
    And reign with Thee above,
Where faith is sweetly lost in sight,
And hope in full supreme delight,
    And everlasting love.

82

ISAIAH 26.13,14

O Lord, my God, with shame I own
    That other lords have swayed,
Have in my heart set up their throne,
    And abject I obeyed.

Thy enemies usurped the place,
    And robbed Thee of Thy due;
A slave to every vice I was,
    And only evil knew.

With sin I joyfully complied,
   I yielded unconstrained;
Passion, and appetite, and pride,
   And self, and nature reigned.

But ended is the shameful hour,
   Th' usurper's reign is past,
Blasted their strength, o'erturned their power,
   And I am saved at last.

Thy love, by which redeemed I am,
   For ever be adored;
I now shall live to bless Thy name,
   And call my Jesus Lord.

Those other lords no more are mine,
   No more their slave am I;
I tread them down with strength divine,
   I all my sins defy.

Freed am I now, for ever freed
   From their destructive power;
Nailed to the cross, they all are dead,
   And shall revive no more.

The glorious presence of my God
   Hath all the tyrants slain;
Their name, their memory is destroyed,
   When I am born again.

83

If for a world a soul be lost,
   Who can the loss supply!
More than a thousand worlds it cost
   One precious soul to buy.

Trust in God

84

MATTHEW 5.3,4,6

Jesu, if still the same Thou art,
 If all Thy promises are sure,
Set up Thy kingdom in my heart,
 And make me rich, for I am poor:
To me be all Thy treasures given,
The kingdom of an inward heaven.

Thou hast pronounced the mourner blest,
 And, lo! for Thee I ever mourn:
I cannot – no! I will not rest,
 Till Thou my only Rest return;
Till Thou, the Prince of Peace, appear.
And I receive the Comforter.

Where is the blessedness bestowed
 On all that hunger after Thee?
I hunger now, I thirst for God!
 See, the poor, fainting sinner see,
And satisfy with endless peace,
And fill me with Thy righteousness.

Ah, Lord! – If Thou art in that sigh,
 Then hear Thyself within me pray.
Hear in my heart Thy Spirit's cry,
 Mark what my labouring soul would say:
Answer the deep, unuttered groan,
And show that Thou and I are one.

Shine on Thy work, disperse the gloom,
  Light in Thy light I then shall see:
Say to my soul, 'Thy light is come,
  Glory divine is risen on thee,
Thy warfare's past, thy mourning's o'er:
Look up; for thou shalt weep no more.'

Lord, I believe the promise sure,
  And trust Thou wilt not long delay;
Hungry, and sorrowful, and poor,
  Upon Thy word myself I stay;
Into Thy hands my all resign,
And wait – till all Thou art is mine!

85

The Lord went before them by day . . .   Exodus 13.21

Captain of Israel's host, and Guide
  Of all who seek that land above,
Beneath Thy shadow we abide,
  The cloud of Thy protecting love,
Our strength Thy grace, our rule Thy word,
Our end, the glory of the Lord.

By Thine unerring Spirit led,
  We shall not in the desert stray,
The light of man's direction need,
  Or miss our providential way,
As far from danger as from fear,
While Love, almighty Love, is near.

Abiding in Christ

86

Abide in me.   John 15.4

I will abide in Thee, my Lord,
   Till life's extremest hour,
For Thou who gav'st the gracious word
   Shalt give the gracious power:
And summoned, with my friends above,
   Thine open face to see,
An age of everlasting love
   I shall abide in Thee.

Following Christ

87

Keep the charge of the Lord, that ye die not.   Leviticus 8.35

A charge to keep I have,
   A God to glorify,
A never-dying soul to save,
   And fit it for the sky;
   To serve the present age,
   My calling to fulfil:
O may it all my powers engage
   To do my Master's will!

Arm me with jealous care,
As in Thy sight to live,
And O! Thy servant, Lord, prepare
A strict account to give:
Help me to watch and pray,
And on Thyself rely,
Assured, if I my trust betray,
I shall for ever die.

88

The fire shall ever be burning upon the altar.   Leviticus 6.13

O Thou who camest from above,
The pure, celestial fire t' impart,
Kindle a flame of sacred love
On the mean altar of my heart;
There let it for Thy glory burn
With inextinguishable blaze,
And trembling to its Source return,
In humble prayer, and fervent praise.

Jesus, confirm my heart's desire
To work, and speak, and think for Thee;
Still let me guard the holy fire,
And still stir up Thy gift in me:
Ready for all Thy perfect will,
My acts of faith and love repeat,
Till death Thy endless mercies seal,
And make my sacrifice complete.

89

I will heal their backsliding . . . Hosea 14.4

How am I healed, if still again
I *must* relapse with grief and pain
  Into my old disease?
If Christ, with all His power and love,
Can never *perfectly* remove
  My desperate wickedness?

But, Lord, I trust, Thy gracious skill
Shall throughly my backslidings heal,
  My sinfulness of soul,
Destroy the bent to sin in me,
Cure my original malady,
  And make, and keep me whole.

90

Whosoever doth not bear his cross, and come after me,
cannot be my disciple Luke 14.27

  Millions the Christian name
   Without the cross receive,
Servants of men and slaves of fame
   In ease and pleasures live;
   Following the world His foe
   They throng the spacious road,
Nor will in Jesu's footsteps go
   By Calvary to God.

But better taught by grace
His doctrines I approve,
Cheerful His daily cross embrace,
And all His sufferings love:
With joy I follow Him
Who once for sinners died,
And nothing know, desire, esteem
But Jesus crucified.

Trial and temptation

91

And did my Lord on earth endure
Sorrow, and hardships, and distress,
That I might sit me down secure,
And rest in self-indulgent ease,
His delicate disciple I
Like Him might neither live, nor die!

Master, I have not learned Thee so:
Thy yoke and burden I receive,
Resolve in all Thy steps to go,
And bless the cross by which I live,
And curse the wisdom from beneath,
That strives to rob me of Thy death.

Thy holy will be done, not mine,
Be suffered all Thy holy will:
I dare not, Lord, the cross decline,
I will not lose the slightest ill,
Or lay the heaviest burden down,
The richest jewel of my crown.

Sorrow is solid joy, and pain
   Is pure delight, endured for Thee;
Reproach and loss are glorious gain,
   And death is immortality;
And who for Thee their all have given,
Have nobly bartered earth for heaven.

Saved is the life for Jesus lost,
   Hidden from earth, but found in God;
To suffer is to triumph most,
   The highest gift on man bestowed;
Seal of my sure election this,
Seal of mine everlasting bliss.

The touchstone, and the proof of grace,
   The standard of perfection here,
The measure of my heavenly place,
   When Christ and all His saints appear,
The mark divine by Jesu's art
Imprinted on my faithful heart.

O might it deeper sink, (but give
   Me strength Thy strongest love to bear,)
Fain would I die with Thee to live,
   Fain would I all Thy passion share;
To me Thy thorny crown be given
On earth, Thy glorious crown in heaven.

IN TEMPTATION

Jesu, Lover of my soul,
  Let me to Thy bosom fly,
While the nearer waters roll,
  While the tempest still is high:
Hide me, O my Saviour, hide,
  Till the storm of life is past;
Safe into the haven guide;
  O, receive my soul at last.

Other refuge have I none,
  Hangs my helpless soul on Thee:
Leave, ah! leave me not alone,
  Still support and comfort me.
All my trust on Thee is stayed;
  All my help from Thee I bring;
Cover my defenceless head
  With the shadow of Thy wing.

Wilt Thou not regard my call?
  Wilt Thou not accept my prayer?
Lo! I sink, I faint, I fall –
  Lo! on Thee I cast my care:
Reach me out Thy gracious hand!
  While I of Thy strength receive,
Hoping against hope I stand,
  Dying, and, behold, I live!

Thou, O Christ, art all I want,
   More than all in Thee I find:
Raise the fallen, cheer the faint,
   Heal the sick, and lead the blind.
Just and holy is Thy name,
   I am all unrighteousness;
False and full of sin I am,
   Thou art full of truth and grace.

Plenteous grace with Thee is found,
   Grace to cover all my sin:
Let the healing streams abound,
   Make and keep me pure within.
Thou of life the Fountain art:
   Freely let me take of Thee,
Spring Thou up within my heart,
   Rise to all eternity!

93

*The jailor . . . thrust them into the inner prison, and made their feet fast in the
stocks.* Acts 16.23,4

Numbered with the transgressors see
   The faithful followers of the Lamb!
Partakers of His infamy
   They glory in the sacred shame,
His bonds and stripes with joy abide,
And bow to Jesus crucified.

How beautiful their feet appear,
   When fettered for their Saviour's sake!
His people's Strength and Comforter
   Doth on Himself their burden take;
And in the dungeon's deepest gloom
Their joy is full, their Light is come!

94

The whole armour of God. Ephesians 6.13

Soldiers of Christ, arise,
    And put your armour on,
Strong in the strength which God supplies
    Through His eternal Son;
    Strong in the Lord of hosts,
    And in His mighty power,
Who in the strength of Jesus trusts
    Is more than conqueror.

Stand then in His great might,
    With all His strength endued,
And take, to arm you for the fight,
    The panoply of God;
    That having all things done,
    And all your conflicts past,
Ye may o'ercome through Christ alone,
    And stand entire at last.

Stand then against your foes,
    In close and firm array;
Legions of wily fiends oppose
    Throughout the evil day;
    But meet the sons of night,
    But mock their vain design,
Armed in the arms of heavenly light,
    Of righteousness divine.

Leave no unguarded place,
　　No weakness of the soul,
Take every virtue, every grace,
　　And fortify the whole;
　　Indissolubly joined,
　　To battle all proceed;
But arm yourselves with all the mind
　　That was in Christ your Head.

Let truth the girdle be,
　　That binds your armour on,
In faithful, firm sincerity
　　To Jesus cleave alone.
　　Let faith and love combine
　　To guard your valiant breast:
The plate be righteousness divine,
　　Imputed, and impressed.

Still let your feet be shod,
　　Ready His will to do,
Ready in all the ways of God
　　His glory to pursue:
　　Ruin is spread beneath,
　　The gospel greaves put on,
And safe through all the snares of death
　　To life eternal run.

But above all, lay hold
　　On faith's victorious shield,
Armed with that adamant, and gold,
　　Be sure to win the field;
　　If faith surround your heart,
　　Satan shall be subdued;
Repelled his every fiery dart,
　　And quenched with Jesu's blood.

Jesus hath died for you!
What can His love withstand?
Believe; hold fast your shield; and who
Shall pluck you from His hand?
Believe, that Jesus reigns,
All power to Him is given;
Believe, till freed from sin's remains,
Believe yourselves to heaven.

Your Rock can never shake:
Hither, He saith, come up!
The helmet of salvation take,
The confidence of hope:
Hope for His perfect love,
Hope for His people's rest,
Hope to sit down with Christ above,
And share the marriage feast.

Brandish in faith till then
The Spirit's two-edged sword,
Hew all the snares of fiends and men
In pieces with the word;
'Tis written; This applied
Baffles their strength and art;
Spirit and soul with this divide,
And joints and marrow part.

To keep your armour bright,
Attend with constant care,
Still walking in your Captain's sight,
And watching unto prayer;
Ready for all alarms,
Steadfastly set your face,
And always exercise your arms,
And use your every grace.

Pray, without ceasing pray,
    (Your Captain gives the word,)
His summons cheerfully obey,
    And call upon the Lord;
    To God your every want
    In instant prayer display,
Pray always; pray, and never faint,
    Pray, without ceasing pray.

In fellowship; alone,
    To God with faith draw near,
Approach His courts, besiege His throne
    With all the powers of prayer:
    Go to His temple, go,
    Nor from His altar move;
Let every house His worship know,
    And every heart His love.

To God your spirits dart,
    Your souls in words declare,
Or groan, to Him who reads the heart,
    Th' unutterable prayer.
    His mercy now implore,
    And now show forth His praise,
In shouts, or silent awe, adore
    His miracles of grace.

Pour out your souls to God,
    And bow them with your knees,
And spread your hearts and hands abroad,
    And pray for Sion's peace;
    Your guides, and brethren, bear
    For ever on your mind;
Extend the arms of mighty prayer,
    Ingrasping all mankind.

From strength to strength go on,
　　Wrestle, and fight, and pray,
Tread all the powers of darkness down,
　　And win the well-fought day;
　　　Still let the Spirit cry
　　　In all His soldiers, 'Come,'
Till Christ the Lord descends from high,
　　And takes the conquerors home.

95

Captain, we look to Thee,
　　Thy promised succours claim,
Humbly assured of victory
　　Through Thine almighty name:
　　　With furious beasts to fight,
　　　Forth in Thy strength we go,
With all the earth-born sons of night.
　　With all the fiends below.

Hold of Thine arm we take,
　　And fearlessly march on,
The world, the realm of Satan, shake,
　　And turn it upside down;
　　　'Gainst all the powers of hell
　　　Undaunted we proceed,
Resistless and invincible
　　Through our triumphant Head.

A suffering fight we wage
With man's oppressive power,
Endure the persecutor's rage,
    Till all the storm is o'er:
    Armed with the patient mind
    Which in our Saviour was,
We bear the hate of all mankind,
    And glory in the cross.

To gain that heavenly prize
We gladly suffer here,
And languish in yon opening skies
    To see His sign appear:
    His sign we soon shall see,
    The Lord shall quickly come,
And give the final victory,
    And take the conquerors home.

96

Ye servants of God, Your Master proclaim,
And publish abroad His wonderful name:
The name all-victorious Of Jesus extol;
His kingdom is glorious, And rules over all.

The waves of the sea Have lift up their voice,
Sore troubled that we In Jesus rejoice;
The floods they are roaring, But Jesus is here,
While we are adoring He always is near.

Men, devils engage, The billows arise,
And horribly rage, And threaten the skies:
Their fury shall never Our steadfastness shock,
The weakest believer Is built on a rock.

God ruleth on high, Almighty to save,
And still He is nigh, His presence we have;
The great congregation His triumph shall sing,
Ascribing salvation To Jesus our King.

Salvation to God Who sits on the throne!
Let all cry aloud, And honour the Son!
Our Jesus's praises The angels proclaim,
Fall down on their faces, And worship the Lamb.

Then let us adore, And give Him His right,
All glory, and power, And wisdom, and might,
All honour and blessing, With angels above,
And thanks never ceasing, And infinite love.

Prayer and the Scriptures

97

O Thou, to whom all hearts are known,
    My latest wish, my one desire
Breathed in the Spirit of thy Son
    Accept, and grant what I require:

Pardon for my offences past,
    Grace for a few good days to come,
Love, the sure pledge of heaven at last,
    And a smooth passage to the tomb.

Two men went up into the temple to pray . . . Luke 18.10

When to the house of prayer we go,
   Who can our secret motive tell?
Beneath the same religious show
   Our good or evil we conceal;
God only knows our inward parts,
The pride, or hunger of our hearts.

The proud He doth far off behold,
   But hears the trembling sinner's prayer,
Pities a soul to Satan sold,
   Who from the confines of despair
In Jesus' name for mercy cries;
And lives – because his Saviour dies!

The written word, entire and pure,
The word which always shall endure,
   My rule of faith and life I own;
Not reason or tradition vain,
Not the authority of man,
   Not an internal light alone.

Built, through the sacred oracles,
On Christ, the Rock that never fails,
   Religion from the fountain brought
I find it in the heavenly book,
What Moses and the prophets spoke,
   What Christ and His apostles taught.

100

When quiet in my house I sit,
　　Thy book be my companion still,
My joy Thy sayings to repeat,
　　Talk o'er the records of Thy will,
And search the oracles divine,
Till every heartfelt word is mine.

101

He expounded unto them in all the scriptures the things concerning himself.
Luke 24.27

The Scriptures all with Christ are filled,
　　With Jesus, and His will to save,
His birth and death are there revealed,
　　His rise and triumph o'er the grave,
His kingdom come in gracious power,
His reign when time shall be no more.

Jesus, divine Interpreter,
　　To me Thine oracles unseal,
Then shall I find and taste Thee there,
　　Thy truth, and power, and mercy feel,
And nothing know, and nothing see
In all the book of God but Thee.

To me that Spirit of wisdom give
  Who doth in all Thy members breathe,
Thy sinless life I then shall live,
  And daily die Thy blessed death,
Fixed in my heart Thy kingdom own,
And rise to Thine eternal throne.

102

They seeing see not; and hearing they hear not.   Matthew 13.13

Saviour I still to Thee apply,
  Before I read or hear,
Creator of the seeing eye,
  And of the hearing ear:
The understanding heart bestow,
  The wisdom from above,
So shall I all Thy doctrines know,
  And all Thy sayings love.

103

WRITTEN IN A BIBLE

Jesu, dear redeeming Lamb,
Show me my own worthless name
Written in the book of God,
Written with Thy precious blood.

Let me here my title see,
To eternal life and Thee;
See and taste how good Thou art,
Find Thy Spirit in my heart.

Then reveal Thy perfect love,
Write me in Thy book above;
Thou who hast my sins forgiven,
Write my worthless name in heaven.

Love, joy, peace

104

DESIRING TO LOVE

O Love divine, how sweet Thou art!
When shall I find my willing heart
   All taken up by Thee!
I thirst, and faint, and die to prove
The greatness of redeeming love,
   The love of Christ to me.

Stronger His love than death or hell;
Its riches are unsearchable;
   The first-born sons of light
Desire in vain its depth to see,
They cannot reach the mystery,
   The length, and breadth, and height.

God only knows the love of God;
O that it now were shed abroad
   In this poor stony heart!
For love I sigh, for love I pine:
This only portion, Lord, be mine,
   Be mine this better part.

O that I could for ever sit,
With Mary at the Master's feet!
  Be this my happy choice,
My only care, delight, and bliss,
My joy, my heaven on earth be this
  To hear the Bridegroom's voice.

O that with humbled Peter I
Could weep, believe, and thrice reply
  My faithfulness to prove,
Thou know'st, (for all to Thee is known,)
Thou know'st, O Lord, and Thou alone,
  Thou know'st that Thee I love.

O that I could with favoured John
Recline my weary head upon
  The dear Redeemer's breast!
From care, and sin, and sorrow free,
Give me, O Lord, to find in Thee
  My everlasting rest.

Thy only love do I require,
Nothing in earth beneath desire,
  Nothing in heaven above;
Let earth, and heaven, and all things go,
Give me Thy only love to know,
  Give me Thy only love.

Be careful for nothing.   Philippians 4.6

Most gracious Lord,
Thy kindest word
I joyfully obey;
Hold fast my confidence restored,
And cast my sins away.

No longer I
Lament and sigh,
With guilty fear oppressed;
To me who on Thy love rely,
Whatever is, is best.

In each event,
The kind intent
Of love divine I see,
And mixed with joyful thanks present
My humble prayers to Thee.

Then let Thy peace
My heart possess;
By Thy unspotted mind
Preserve in perfect quietness
A soul to Jesus joined.

In spirit one
With Christ Thy Son,
Henceforth His life I live,
Till Jesus claim me for His own,
And to His arms receive.

106

O what shall I do, My Saviour to praise,
So faithful and true, So plenteous in grace;
So strong to deliver, So good to redeem
The weakest believer That hangs upon Him!

How happy the man Whose heart is set free,
The people that can Be joyful in Thee!
Their joy is to walk in The light of Thy face,
And still they are talking of Jesus's grace.

Their daily delight Shall be in Thy name,
They shall as their right Thy righteousness claim:
Thy righteousness wearing, And cleansed by Thy blood,
Bold shall they appear in The presence of God.

For Thou art their boast, Their glory and power;
And I also trust To see the glad hour,
My soul's new creation, A life from the dead,
The day of salvation That lifts up my head.

For Jesus my Lord Is now my defence,
I trust in His word, None plucks me from thence:
Since I have found favour He all things will do,
My King and my Saviour Shall make me anew.

Yes, Lord, I shall see The bliss of Thine own,
Thy secret to me Shall soon be made known,
For sorrow and sadness I joy shall receive,
And share in the gladness of all that believe.

Fountain of endless mercies,
  Giver of all in Jesus,
    Who from Thy throne
    Hast sent Thy Son
To ransom and to bless us:
Respect our humble mansion
  With grateful joy resounding,
    With hymns of praise
    For pardoning grace
Above our sins abounding.

Acknowledging the Author
  And God of our salvation,
    Our hearts we lift,
    And own the gift
Too mighty for expression:
We would be truly thankful
  Whom Jesus doth deliver
    From all our foes,
    And peace bestows,
And life that lasts for ever.

At morning, noon, and evening
  Our sacrifices bringing,
    We instantly
    Give praise to Thee,
The song triumphant singing;
With all Thy ransomed people
  Through Jesus' blood forgiven,
    From earth we fly,
    And scale the sky,
And join the choir of heaven.

6 One-minute Meditations

On some words of Scripture

Whole chapters (in one case, a whole book) have been written describing and illustrating the familiarity of the Wesleys with the Scriptures. Dr Bett describes how he tested three chapters, taken at random, where in his *Notes on the New Testament* John Wesley introduced sixty-one changes into the Authorized Version translation – and found that in over half of them he anticipated the identical changes published in the Revised Version of 1881, over a century later.

Already in this small anthology the same truth will have become apparent in Charles Wesley's hymns. 'His verse is an enormous sponge filled to saturation with Bible words, Bible similes, Bible metaphors, Bible stories, Bible themes,' writes Frank Baker. He cites the verdict of Dr J. E. Rattenbury, 'A skilful man, if the Bible were lost, might extract much of it from Wesley's hymns. They contain the Bible in solution.' The Index of Scriptural Allusions in the latest critical edition of John Wesley's original 1780 *Collection* contains some two and a half thousand entries, including every book of the Bible save two – the prophet Nahum and the letter to Philemon. Many of these entries refer to up to a dozen different hymns – and the *Collection*, of course, contains only a fraction of Charles Wesley's published verse!

The ten 'meditations' in this section are taken mainly from one or other of the two volumes entitled *Short Hymns on Select Passages of the Holy Scriptures* published in 1762, and containing 2,348 'hymns'; while when Dr Osborne prepared his *Poetical Works* in 1868–72 he added to this number to make a total of 3,491. Other examples are to be found in this anthology grouped under appropriate subject headings. In spite of the title the author gave them, it is clear that few of these are 'hymns' in the usual meaning of the word, namely (as defined by the *Oxford English Dictionary*) 'a metrical composition adapted to be sung in a religious service'. Earlier volumes of his work had borne the double description 'Hymns and Sacred Poems', but by this time the effort to differentiate between them had been abandoned. None of these found a place in the 1780 *Collection*; and it is difficult to think of most of them being sung as hymns except upon some very particular occasion.

But, especially to an earlier generation, hymns were not confined solely to congregational use. The hymns of Methodism have nourished individual devotion since the days when they were written, and do so still today. When Lord Tonypandy, in the radio programme 'Desert Island Discs', was asked by Roy Plomley what book he would choose to take to a desert island (already thoughtfully provided with the Bible and the works of Shakespeare) he spoke for many Christians in his choice of the Methodist Hymn Book.

In his Preface to the first edition Charles Wesley explained how it was owing to ill-health and enforced inactivity that this great profusion of short hymns or poems, meditative and often epigrammatical, came to be written. He went on to explain his concern for the truths of the gospel, especially for a right understanding of Christian holiness, concluding:

> Reader, if God ministers grace to thy soul through any of these hymns, give Him the glory, and offer up a prayer for the weak instrument, that, whenever I finish my course, I may depart in peace, having seen in JESUS CHRIST His great salvation.

108

They heard the voice of the Lord God walking in the garden in the cool of the day. Genesis 3.8

Not on the whirlwind's wings He flies,
   Not in the thunder's voice He speaks,
But that the fallen man may rise,
   The Lord His ruined creature seeks:
Not in the burning blaze of day,
   (For fury hath no place in Him,)
But placid as the evening ray,
   He comes, to sentence, and redeem.

109

Forgive, I pray thee, my sin only this once. Exodus 10.17

Times without number have I prayed,
   This only once forgive,
Relapsing, when Thy hand was stayed
   And suffered me to live:
Yet now the kingdom of Thy peace,
   Lord, to my heart restore,
Forgive my vain repentances,
   And bid me sin no more.

110

The waters that were in the river were turned to blood. Exodus 7.20

He turned their water into blood,
  When vengeance was His dread design:
But, thanks to the incarnate God,
  He turned our water into wine!

111

When I saw . . . then I coveted them, and took them. Joshua 7.21

'I saw, and coveted, and took!'
  The progress this of every sin;
While death, admitted by a look,
  Lets everlasting judgments in:
But if an eye of faith on Thee
  I turn, directed by Thy word,
Jesus mine Advocate I see,
  I see, desire, and take my Lord.

112

Oh that I knew where I might find him! Job 23.3

Where but on yonder tree?
  Or if too rich thou art,
    Sink into poverty,
And find Him in thine heart.

I have graven thee upon the palms of my hands.   Isaiah 49.16

Engraven with an iron pen
My name upon Thy hands is seen:
Lord, with Thy love's acutest dart
Engrave Thy name upon my heart.

114

We are the clay, and thou our potter.   Isaiah 64.8

My Potter from above,
Clay in Thy hands I am,
Mould me into the form of love,
And stamp with Thy new name:
Thy name is holiness;
Now on this heart of mine
The mark indelible impress,
The purity divine.

115

Take my yoke upon you, and learn of me.   Matthew 11.29

Lord, I fain would learn of Thee
Meekness and humility;
In Thy gentleness of mind
In Thy lowliness of heart
Rest mine inmost soul shall find,
Rest that never can depart.

Jesus . . . saw two brethren . . . casting a net into the sea.   Matthew 4.18

The schools of scribes, and courts of kings,
　　The learn'd and great He passes by,
Chooses the weak and foolish things,
　　His power and grace to testify;
Plain simple men His call endues
　　With power and wisdom from above;
And such He still vouchsafes to use,
　　Who nothing know but Jesus' love.

117

And they all wept sore.   Acts 20.37

Jesus wept! and never chid
　　Tears of social tenderness;
Saints are not by Him forbid
　　Thus their frailty to confess,
Thus by passion pure to prove
Saints are men of grief and love.

For other similar 'one-minute meditations' see Nos. 7, 12, 27, 28, 42, 43, 44, 62, 63, 80, 100, 102, 118, 124, 125.

7 Each Returning Day

The new day · Grace at table · Daily work · In a storm
The child and the family · Music · Evening

Charles Wesley married at the age of forty-two, having been for ten years a field preacher. His married home was in Bristol, and here he and his Sarah lived for twenty-two years. Eight children were born to them, of whom five died in infancy; Charles junior, their eldest son, inherited the musical gifts of both his parents, and the *Dictionary of National Biography* says of him that at the age of two and three-quarters he could play 'a tune on the harpsichord readily and in just time', and even 'always put a true bass to it'. Sadly, it goes on to describe him as 'perhaps the most singular instance on record of altogether exceptional musical precocity leading to no great results in after life.'

It is with these domesticities in mind that I have included in this section verses about music and about family life. 'The true use of Music', *129*, was by tradition written by Charles Wesley after an open-air service in a sea-port had been rudely interrupted by a company of half-drunken sailors (some accounts say soldiers) singing a lewd song called 'Nancy Dawson'. Charles mastered the tune, and at the following service had the people sing to it these new words. The tune in question seems to have been a version of 'Here we go round the mulberry bush' – and it is an example of Charles Wesley's versatility that he should have written to order with such apparent ease and finish in a metre unlike those in which he was usually working.

Two of the hymns in this section remain in constant use for the worship of the Church. 'Forth in thy name', (*121*), lends itself uniquely to many occasions of conclusion or departure; while 'Christ, whose glory fills the skies' (*119*) appears in the latest Methodist hymn book and in the latest edition of

Hymns Ancient and Modern (both 1983) exactly as it was first written.

I have included the verses of 'In a storm' (*123*), as a reminder of the days of Charles Wesley's itinerant ministry. Though the imagery is drawn from a storm at sea (such as he experienced in his Atlantic crossings and his visits to Ireland) rough weather must have been part of his regular experience not only in his days as field preacher, but even after his marriage as he assisted his brother with 'the care of all the churches', Sarah sometimes riding behind him on his horse. It was his custom to compose his hymns on horseback; and Henry Moore in his *Life* of 1825 has left us this picture of the poet in old age:

> When he was nearly fourscore, he retained something of this eccentricity. He rode every day, (clothed for winter even in summer,) a little horse, grey with age. When he mounted, if a subject struck him, he proceeded to expand, and put it in order. He would write a hymn thus given him, on a card, (kept for the purpose,) with his pencil, in short-hand. Not unfrequently he has come to our house in the City-road, and, having left the poney in the *garden* in front, he would enter, crying out, 'Pen and ink! Pen and ink!' These being supplied, he wrote the hymn he had been composing. When this was done, he would look round on those present, and salute them with much kindness, ask after their health, give out a short hymn, and thus put all in mind of eternity.

The new day

118

I was in the Spirit on the Lord's day.   Revelation 1.10

May I throughout this day of Thine
  Be in Thy Spirit, Lord,
Spirit of humble fear divine
  That trembles at Thy word,
Spirit of faith my heart to raise,
  And fix on things above,
Spirit of sacrifice and praise,
  Of holiness and love.

119

Christ, whose glory fills the skies,
  Christ, the true, the only Light,
Sun of Righteousness, arise,
  Triumph o'er the shades of night;
Dayspring from on high, be near;
Daystar, in my heart appear.

Dark and cheerless is the morn,
  Unaccompanied by Thee:
Joyless is the day's return,
  Till Thy mercy's beams I see;
Till they inward light impart,
Glad my eyes, and warm my heart.

Visit, then, this soul of mine,
    Pierce the gloom of sin and grief;
Fill me, Radiancy divine,
    Scatter all my unbelief,
More and more Thyself display,
Shining to the perfect day.

Grace at table

120

Glory, love, and praise, and honour
        For our food
        Now bestowed
Render we the Donor.
Bounteous God, we now confess Thee;
        God, who thus
        Blessest us,
Meet it is to bless Thee.

Knows the ox his master's stable,
        And shall we
        Not know Thee,
Nourished at Thy table?
Yes, of all good gifts the Giver
        Thee we own,
        Thee alone
Magnify for ever.

Daily work

121

Forth in Thy name, O Lord, I go,
  My daily labour to pursue,
Thee, only Thee resolved to know
  In all I think, or speak, or do.

The task Thy wisdom hath assigned
  O let me cheerfully fulfil,
In all my works Thy presence find,
  And prove Thine acceptable will.

Preserve me from my calling's snare,
  And hide my simple heart above,
Above the thorns of choking care,
  The gilded baits of worldly love.

Thee may I set at my right hand,
  Whose eyes mine inmost substance see,
And labour on at Thy command,
  And offer all my works to Thee.

Give me to bear Thy easy yoke,
  And every moment watch and pray,
And still to things eternal look,
  And hasten to Thy glorious day.

For Thee delightfully employ
  Whate'er Thy bounteous grace hath given,
And run my course with even joy,
  And closely walk with Thee to heaven.

TO BE SUNG AT WORK

Son of the carpenter, receive
    This humble work of mine;
Worth to my meanest labour give,
    By joining it to Thine.

Servant of all, to toil for man
    Thou wouldst not, Lord, refuse:
Thy Majesty did not disdain
    To be employed for us.

Thy bright example I pursue,
    To Thee in all things rise,
And all I think, or speak, or do,
    Is one great sacrifice.

Careless through outward cares I go,
    From all distraction free:
My hands are but engaged below,
    My heart is still with Thee.

O, when wilt Thou, my Life, appear!
    How gladly would I cry,
'''Tis done, the work Thou gav'st me here,
    'Tis finished, Lord,' – and die!

123

Glory to Thee, whose powerful word
   Bids the tempestuous wind arise;
Glory to Thee, the sovereign Lord
   Of air, and earth, and seas, and skies!

Let air, and earth, and skies obey,
   And seas Thy awful will perform:
From them we learn to own Thy sway,
   And shout to meet the gathering storm.

What though the floods lift up their voice,
   Thou hearest, Lord, our louder cry;
They cannot damp Thy children's joys,
   Or shake the soul, when God is nigh.

Headlong we cleave the yawning deep.
   And back to highest heaven are borne,
Unmoved, though rapid whirlwinds sweep,
   And all the watery world upturn.

Roar on, ye waves! Our souls defy
   Your roaring to disturb our rest:
In vain t' impair the calm ye try,
   The calm in a believer's breast.

Rage, while our faith the Saviour tries,
   Thou sea, the servant of His will:
Rise, while our God permits thee, rise;
   But fall, when He shall say, 'Be still!'

The child and the family

124

He took a child, and set him in the midst . . . Mark 9.36

Who would not eagerly desire
    That envied infant's place?
Jesus, I to Thine arms aspire,
    And pant for Thy embrace:
My ruined innocence re-give,
    My lost simplicity,
And then with arms of love receive
    A little child in me.

125

He took them up in his arms . . . Mark 10.16

Who is this condescending Friend,
    That doth for children care,
That doth my little ones defend,
    And in His bosom bear?
The arms, within whose soft embrace
    My sleeping babes I see,
They comprehend unbounded space,
    And grasp infinity!

Lover of little children, Thee,
  O Jesus, we adore;
Our kind and loving Saviour be,
  Both now and evermore.

O take us up into Thine arms,
  And we are truly blessed;
Thy new-born babes are safe from harms,
  While harboured in Thy breast.

There let us ever, ever sleep,
  Strangers to guilt and care;
Free from the world of evil, keep
  Our tender spirits there.

Still, as we grow in years, in grace
  And wisdom let us grow;
But never leave Thy dear embrace,
  But never evil know.

Strong let us in Thy grace abide,
  But ignorant of ill;
In malice, subtlety, and pride
  Let us be children still.

Lover of little children, Thee,
  O Jesus, we adore;
Our kind and loving Saviour be
  Both now and evermore.

PART I

Gentle Jesus, meek and mild,
Look upon a little child;
Pity my simplicity,
Suffer me to come to Thee.

Fain I would to Thee be brought;
Dearest God, forbid it not;
Give me, dearest God, a place
In the kingdom of Thy grace.

Put Thy hands upon my head;
Let me in Thine arms be stayed;
Let me lean upon Thy breast;
Lull me, lull me, Lord, to rest.

Hold me fast in Thine embrace,
Let me see Thy smiling face;
Give me, Lord, Thy blessing give;
Pray for me, and I shall live:

I shall live the simple life,
Free from sin's uneasy strife;
Sweetly ignorant of ill,
Innocent and happy still.

O that I may never know
What the wicked people do!
Sin is contrary to Thee,
Sin is the forbidden tree.

Keep me from the great offence,
Guard my helpless innocence;
Hide me, from all evil hide,
Self, and stubbornness, and pride.

PART II

Lamb of God, I look to Thee,
Thou shalt my example be:
Thou art gentle, meek, and mild,
Thou wast once a little child.

Fain I would be as Thou art;
Give me Thy obedient heart;
Thou art pitiful and kind,
Let me have Thy loving mind.

Meek and lowly may I be;
Thou art all humility:
Let me to my betters bow,
Subject to Thy parents Thou.

Let me, above all, fulfil
God my heavenly Father's will;
Never His good Spirit grieve,
Only to His glory live.

Thou didst live to God alone,
Thou didst never seek Thine own,
Thou Thyself didst never please,
God was all Thy happiness.

Loving Jesus, gentle Lamb!
In Thy gracious hands I am;
Make me, Saviour, what Thou art;
Live Thyself within my heart.

I shall then show forth Thy praise,
Serve Thee all my happy days:
Then the world shall always see
Christ, the holy Child, in me.

128

ON SENDING A CHILD TO THE BOARDING-SCHOOL

Not without Thy direction
    From us our child we send,
And to Thy sure protection
    Her innocence commend:
Jesus, Thou Friend and Lover
    Of helpless infancy,
With wings of mercy cover
    A soul beloved by Thee.

Evil communication
    O let it not pervert,
Or fill with pride and passion
    Her fond unwary heart;
Preserve her uninfected
    (In answer to our prayers)
From dangers unsuspected,
    From twice ten thousand snares.

Let no affections foolish
    Or vain her spirit soil;
Let no instructions polish
    Her nature into guile;
No low dissimulation
    Place in her bosom find,
No worldly art of fashion
    Corrupt her simple mind.

Our little one, believing,
    Beneath Thy care we place,
And see Thee, Lord, receiving
    Her into Thine embrace:
Thyself her inward Teacher,
    Thyself her Guardian be,
And graciously enrich her
    With all that is in Thee.

Music

129

THE TRUE USE OF MUSIC

Listed into the cause of sin,
    Why should a good be evil?
Music, alas! too long has been
    Pressed to obey the devil:
Drunken, or lewd, or light the lay
    Flowed to the soul's undoing,
Widened, and strewed with flowers the way
    Down to eternal ruin.

Who on the part of God will rise,
    Innocent sound recover,
Fly on the prey, and take the prize,
    Plunder the carnal lover,
Strip him of every moving strain,
    Every melting measure,
Music in virtue's cause retain,
    Rescue the holy pleasure?

Come let us try if Jesu's love
    Will not as well inspire us:
This is the theme of those above,
    This upon earth shall fire us.
Say, if your hearts are tuned to sing,
    Is there a subject greater?
Harmony all its strains may bring,
    Jesus's name is sweeter.

Jesus the soul of music is;
    His is the noblest passion:
Jesus's name is joy and peace,
    Happiness and salvation:
Jesus's name the dead can raise,
    Show us our sins forgiven,
Fill us with all the life of grace,
    Carry us up to heaven.

Who hath a right like us to sing,
    Us whom His mercy raises?
Merry our hearts, for Christ is King,
    Cheerful are all our faces:
Who of His love doth once partake
    He evermore rejoices:
Melody in our hearts we make,
    Melody with our voices.

He that a sprinkled conscience hath,
    He that in God is merry,
Let him sing psalms, the Spirit saith,
    Joyful, and never weary,
Offer the sacrifice of praise,
    Hearty, and never ceasing,
Spiritual songs and anthems raise,
    Honour, and thanks, and blessing.

Then let us in His praises join,
    Triumph in His salvation,
Glory ascribe to love divine,
    Worship, and adoration:
Heaven already is begun,
    Opened in each believer;
Only believe, and still sing on,
    Heaven is ours for ever.

130

THE MUSICIAN'S HYMN

Thou God of harmony and love,
Whose name transports the saints above,
    And lulls the ravished spheres:
On Thee in feeble strains I call,
And mix my humble voice with all
    The heavenly choristers.

If well I know the tuneful art
To captivate a human heart,
  The glory, Lord, be Thine:
A servant of Thy blessed will,
I here devote my utmost skill
  To sound the praise divine.

With Tubal's wretched sons no more
I prostitute my sacred power,
  To please the fiends beneath;
Or modulate the wanton lay,
Or smooth with music's hand the way
  To everlasting death.

Suffice for this the season past:
I come, great God, to learn at last
  The lesson of Thy grace;
Teach me the new, the gospel song,
And let my hand, my heart, my tongue,
  Move only to Thy praise.

Thine own musician, Lord, inspire,
And let my consecrated lyre
  Repeat the psalmist's part:
His Son and Thine reveal in me,
And fill with sacred melody
  The fibres of my heart.

So shall I charm the listening throng,
And draw the living stones along,
  By Jesu's tuneful name:
The living stones shall dance, shall rise,
And form a city in the skies,
  The new Jerusalem!

O might I with Thy saints aspire,
The meanest of that dazzling choir,
    Who chant Thy praise above;
Mixed with the bright musician-band,
May I an heavenly harper stand,
    And sing the song of love.

What ecstasy of bliss is there,
While all th' angelic concert share,
    And drink the floating joys!
What more than ecstasy, when all
Struck to the golden pavement fall
    At Jesu's glorious voice!

Jesus, the heaven of heaven He is,
The soul of harmony and bliss!
    And while on Him we gaze,
And while His glorious voice we hear,
Our spirits are all eye, all ear,
    And silence speaks His praise.

O might I die that awe to prove,
That prostrate awe which dares not move,
    Before the great Three-One;
To shout by turns the bursting joy,
And all eternity employ
    In songs around the throne.

Evening

131

Thou, Lord, art rich in grace to all,
    Attend my earnest cry,
With lifted hands and heart I call,
    And look to feel Thee nigh.

O that my prayers might now to Thee
    As clouds of incense rise,
And let my thanks accepted be,
    My evening sacrifice.

Not unto me, O Lord, the praise,
    But to Thy name I give,
If kept by Thine almighty grace,
    Still unconsumed I live.

Through Thee, my God, through Thee alone
    I incorrupt have been,
Thou hast Thy power in weakness shown,
    Withholding me from sin.

Restrained from my own wickedness,
    Thy outstretched arm I see,
And bless Thee for my faith's increase,
    And closer cleave to Thee.

With humble thankfulness I own,
    Sufficient is Thy grace,
Thou who from sin hast kept me one,
    Canst keep me all my days.

8 Death and Heaven

Friends above · For one departing · Condemned prisoners
After the funeral · Rejoice for a brother deceased
Lines dictated on his deathbed · A Christian's epitaph

In such a fellowship as early Methodism, at once widespread
and close-knit, death was an ever-present reality; and heaven
correspondingly a firmer and brighter hope. Charles Wesley
wrote very many funeral hymns sounding the authentic Christian note of triumph. John Wesley once exclaimed, 'Oh, what
would Dr Watts have said if he had lived to see my brother's
two exquisite *Funeral Hymns*, beginning "How happy every
child of grace" and "Come, let us join our friends above"?' It
was this latter hymn, (*132*), which John Wesley and his congregation were singing in Staffordshire as Charles lay dying;
and *133* that John Wesley's friends sang standing round his
death bed at City Road. The last verse of *136* was often
Charles's own choice when in old age he called a group of
believers to an informal chorus of praise.

The cause of prisoners under sentence of death was dear to
Charles Wesley's heart. The first reference in his *Journal* dates
back to 10 July, 1738, only weeks after his conversion. He
ministered the gospel faithfully and with power to a group of
ten in Newgate, including a black prisoner, for a little over a
week; seeing the dawn of saving faith and joyful assurance. His
Journal for 19 July (here abbreviated) describes their execution:

> Wed., July 19th, I rose very heavy, and backward to visit
> them for the last time. At six I prayed and sang with them all
> together. All the ten received [Holy Communion].
>   At half-hour past nine their irons were knocked off, and
> their hands tied. By half-hour past ten we came to Tyburn,
> waited till eleven: then were brought the children appointed
> to die. I got upon the cart: the Ordinary endeavoured to

follow, when the poor prisoners begged he might not come; and the mob kept him down.

I prayed first. We had prayed before that our Lord would show there was a power superior to the fear of death. They were all cheerful; full of comfort, peace, and triumph; assuredly persuaded Christ had died for them, and waited to receive them into paradise.

The Black had spied me coming out of the coach, and saluted me with his looks. As often as his eyes met mine, he smiled with the most composed, delightful countenance I ever saw. None showed any natural terror of death: no fear, or crying, or tears. All expressed their desire of our following them to paradise. I never saw such calm triumph, such incredible indifference to dying. We sang several hymns . . .

We left them going to meet their Lord, ready for the Bridegroom. When the cart drew off, not one stirred, or struggled for life, but meekly gave up their spirits. Exactly at twelve they were turned off. I spoke a few suitable words to the crowd; and returned, full of peace and confidence in our friends' happiness. That hour under the gallows was the most blessed hour of my life.

The final two items are Charles's last composition, and his epitaph. He dictated *137* to his wife 'when he came in faint and drooping from taking an airing in a coach, a few days before his end'. The final epitaph, written by him for another, can be seen today on Charles Wesley's memorial, an obelisk in a little garden off Marylebone High Street in London, replacing the original tombstone in Marylebone churchyard where he was buried on 5 April, 1788.

FRIENDS ABOVE

Come let us join our friends above
    That have obtained the prize,
And on the eagle wings of love
    To joy celestial rise;
Let all the saints terrestrial sing
    With those to glory gone,
For all the servants of our King
    In earth and heaven are one.

One family we dwell in Him,
    One church above, beneath,
Though now divided by the stream,
    The narrow stream of death:
One army of the living God,
    To His command we bow:
Part of His host hath crossed the flood,
    And part is crossing now.

Ten thousand to their endless home
    This solemn moment fly,
And we are to the margin come,
    And we expect to die:
His militant, embodied host,
    With wishful looks we stand,
And long to see that happy coast,
    And reach that heavenly land.

Our old companions in distress
   We haste again to see,
And eager long for our release
   And full felicity:
E'en now by faith we join our hands
   With those that went before,
And greet the blood-besprinkled bands
   On the eternal shore.

Our spirits too shall quickly join,
   Like theirs, with glory crowned,
And shout to see our Captain's sign,
   To hear His trumpet sound:
O that we now might grasp our Guide!
   O that the word were given!
Come, Lord of hosts, the waves divide,
   And land us all in heaven.

133

FOR ONE DEPARTING

Happy soul, thy days are ended,
   All thy mourning days below:
Go, by angel guards attended,
   To the sight of Jesus go!
Waiting to receive thy spirit,
   Lo! the Saviour stands above,
Shows the purchase of His merit,
   Reaches out the crown of love.

Struggle through thy latest passion
   To thy dear Redeemer's breast,
To His uttermost salvation,
   To His everlasting rest:
For the joy He sets before thee,
   Bear a momentary pain,
Die, to live the life of glory,
   Suffer, with thy Lord to reign.

134

CONDEMNED PRISONERS

O let the prisoners' mournful sighs
   Come up before Thy gracious throne,
Mixed with the blood and dying cries
   Of Jesus Thy beloved Son.

Father, regard His powerful prayer,
   Who, hanging on the shameful tree,
Doth all our sins and sorrows bear,
   And look, through Jesu's wounds, on me!

On us the outcasts of mankind,
   Who judge ourselves not fit to live,
But mercy hope from Thee to find,
   Through Him that gasped in death, Forgive!

Hear Him, our Advocate with Thee,
   Him, and the blood of sprinkling hear;
He poured out all that blood for me!
   He doth before Thy throne appear!

For us He in Thy presence stands,
    For us He prays the ceaseless prayer,
Points to His side, and lifts His hands,
    And shows that I am graven there!

Lo! on Thy Son our souls we cast,
    And trusting what He asks shall be,
And dying penitent at last,
    We leave our cause to Him and Thee!

135

AFTER THE FUNERAL

Come, let us who in Christ believe
    With saints and angels join,
Glory, and praise, and blessing give,
    And thanks, to Love divine.

Our friend in sure and certain hope
    Hath laid his body down;
He knew that Christ shall raise him up,
    And give the starry crown.

To all who His appearing love
    He opens paradise;
And we shall join the hosts above,
    And we shall grasp the prize.

Then let us wait to see the day,
    To hear the joyful word,
To answer, Lo! we come away,
    We die to meet our Lord.

REJOICE FOR A BROTHER DECEASED

Rejoice for a brother deceased,
   (Our loss is his infinite gain,)
A soul out of prison released,
   And freed from its bodily chain:
With songs let us follow his flight,
   And mount with his spirit above,
Escaped to the mansions of light,
   And lodged in the Eden of love.

Our brother the haven hath gained,
   Outflying the tempest and wind,
His rest he hath sooner obtained,
   And left his companions behind;
Still tossed on a sea of distress,
   Hard toiling to make the blest shore,
Where all is assurance and peace,
   And sorrow and sin are no more.

There all the ship's company meet,
   Who sailed with the Saviour beneath;
With shouting each other they greet,
   And triumph o'er trouble and death:
The voyage of life's at an end,
   The mortal affliction is past,
The age that in heaven they spend
   For ever and ever shall last.

137

LINES DICTATED ON HIS DEATH BED

In age and feebleness extreme,
Who shall a helpless worm redeem?
Jesus! my only hope Thou art,
Strength of my failing flesh and heart;
Oh! could I catch one smile from Thee
And drop into eternity!

138

A CHRISTIAN'S EPITAPH

With poverty of spirit blessed,
Rest, happy saint, in Jesus rest;
A sinner saved, through grace forgiven,
Redeemed from earth to reign in heaven!
Thy labours of unwearied love,
By thee forgot, are crowned above;
Crowned, through the mercy of thy Lord,
With a free, full, immense reward!

INDEX OF TITLES AND FIRST LINES

Where a hymn in common use is based on an item listed below, but with a different opening line, the first line of the hymn is included here in quotation marks. Titles similarly appear in italics.

A charge to keep I have *87*
A Christian's epitaph *138*
A monument of mercy's power *14*
A prayer for the bishops *68*
A prayer for the Church of England *55*
After preaching *65*
After preaching in a church *66*
After the funeral *135*
Ah, woe is me, immersed in sin *61*
All ye that pass by *69*
And are we yet alive *46*
And can it be, that I should gain *2*
And did my Lord on earth endure *91*
Author of life divine *71*

Baptized into one only name *40*

Captain of Israel's host, and Guide *85*
Captain, we look to Thee *95*
Catholick love *54*
Christ is the one Foundation laid *56*
Christ the friend of sinners *1*
'Christ the Lord is risen today' *33*
Christ, whose glory fills the skies *119*

Christ's ministers apart are set *62*
Come all the lost race, Redeemed from your fall *70*
Come Holy Ghost, Thine influence shed *74*
Come, let us anew *26*
Come let us join our friends above *132*
Come, let us who in Christ believe *135*
Come, let us with speed To Bethlehem go *24*
Come, O Thou Traveller unknown *3*
Come, Thou long expected Jesus *22*
Condemned prisoners *134*

Desiring to love *104*
Draw near, O Son of God, draw near *68*

Engraven with an iron pen *113*
Entered the holy place above *37*
Eternal Beam of light divine *10*

Father, if I have sinned, with Thee *16*
Father of Jesus Christ our Lord *76*

Father, whose everlasting love *79*
For one departing 133
For the anniversary day of one's conversion 4
Forth in Thy name, O Lord, I go *121*
Fountain of endless mercies *107*
Free grace 2
Friends above 132

Gentle Jesus, meek and mild *127*
Glory, and praise, and love to Thee *65*
Glory, love, and praise, and honour *120*
Glory to God, and praise, and love *4*
Glory to Thee, whose powerful word *123*
God of a truth in us resides *43*
God of all consolation *39*

Hail the day that sees Him rise *36*
Happy soul, thy days are ended *133*
Happy the man to whom 'tis given *73*
Hark how all the welkin rings *25*
'Hark! the herald angels sing' *25*
He loved, and gave Himself for me *30*
He turned their water into blood *110*
Head of Thy Church, attend *55*

Holy Ghost, regard our prayers *60*
How am I healed, if still again *89*
Hymn for Christmas Day 25

'I saw, and coveted, and took!' *111*
I think Him David's Son *6*
I will abide in Thee, my Lord *86*
If for a world a soul be lost *83*
In affliction 10
In age and feebleness extreme *137*
In temptation 92
In that sad memorable night *29*
In the name of the Lord *64*
Isaiah 26.13,14 82

Jesu, accept the grateful song *66*
Jesu, dear redeeming Lamb *103*
Jesu, if still the same Thou art *84*
Jesu, Lover of my soul *92*
Jesu, mighty to deliver *51*
Jesu, my God and King *17*
Jesu, on Thee we feed *75*
Jesus the good Shepherd is *47*
'Jesus the name, high over all' *66*
Jesus, Thy servants bless *59*
Jesus wept! and never chid *117*
Jesus, who is a God like Thee! *12*

'Lamb of God, I look to Thee' *127*

'Let all the saints terrestrial sing' *132*

'Let saints on earth in concert sing' *132*

Lines dictated on his death bed *137*

Listed into the cause of sin *129*

Lo! He comes with clouds descending *21*

Lord, I fain would learn of Thee *115*

Lord of the gospel harvest, send *57*

Love divine, all loves excelling *20*

Lover of little children, Thee *126*

'Love's redeeming work is done' *33*

Matthew 5.3,4,6 *84*

May I throughout this day of Thine *118*

Millions the Christian name *90*

Most gracious Lord *105*

My heart is full of Christ, and longs *49*

My Potter from above *114*

Not on the whirlwind's wings He flies *108*

Not without Thy direction *128*

Numbered with the transgressors see *93*

'O for a thousand tongues to sing' *4*

O for an heart to praise my God *50*

O let the prisoners' mournful sighs *134*

O Lord, my God, with shame I own *82*

O Love divine, how sweet Thou art! *104*

O Love divine, what hast Thou done! *32*

O Thou, to whom all hearts are known *97*

O Thou who camest from above *88*

O what shall I do, My Saviour to praise *106*

On sending a child to the boarding-school *128*

Patient I waited for the Lord *48*

Praise be to the Father given! *41*

Praise the Lord, ye ransomed nations *53*

'Pray, without ceasing pray' *94*

Rejoice for a brother deceased *136*

Rejoice, the Lord is King! *18*

Saviour I still to Thee apply *102*

Shepherd of souls, the great, the good *67*

Soldiers of Christ, arise *94*

Son of the carpenter, receive *122*

Spirit of faith, on Thee we call *38*

Stay, Thou insulted Spirit stay *77*

Stupendous love of God most high! *5*

The breathless body of our
    Lord *35*

The end of sin and death is
    near *9*

The gospel stands in Moses'
    place *78*

The musician's hymn *130*

The one religion see *80*

*The prayer of a departing
    minister* *67*

The schools of scribes, and
    courts of kings *116*

The Scriptures all with Christ
    are filled *101*

The true use of music *129*

The voice of God the Father
    sounds *8*

The written word, entire and
    pure *99*

The Word was independent
    God *7*

Thou God of glorious
    majesty *81*

Thou God of harmony and
    love *130*

Thou hidden Source of calm
    repose *19*

Thou, Lord, art rich in grace to
    all *131*

Times without number have I
    prayed *109*

To be sung at work *122*

To David's Son and sovereign
    Lord *28*

To Father, Son, and Holy
    Ghost *45*

Two and two, not one and
    one *63*

Victim divine, Thy grace we
    claim *72*

Weary of all this wordy
    strife *54*

What doth the ladder mean *15*

When He did our flesh
    assume *23*

When quiet in my house I
    sit *100*

When to the house of prayer we
    go *98*

Where but on yonder
    tree? *112*

Where shall my wondering soul
    begin? *1*

Who but the Holy Ghost can
    make *58*

Who comprehends the reason
    why *31*

Who God in Christ
    discover *13*

Who is this condescending
    Friend *125*

Who Jehovah's mind hath
    known? *42*

Who Moses and the prophets
    hear *27*

Who seek the Crucified *34*

Who sent the Son is true *44*

Who would not eagerly
    desire *124*

With glorious clouds
    encompassed round *11*

With poverty of spirit
    blessed *138*

Wrestling Jacob *3*

Written in a bible *103*

Ye nations, who the globe
    divide *52*

Ye servants of God, Your
    Master proclaim *96*